T0146596

INSPIRED BY
GOD'S WISDOM

MAUREEN MILLAR

BALBOA.
PRESS

A DIVISION OF HAY HOUSE

Balboa Press books may be ordered through booksellers or by contacting:

Balboa Press
A Division of Hay House
1663 Liberty Drive
Bloomington, IN 47403
www.balboapress.com
1 (877) 407-4847

Because of the dynamic nature of the Internet, any web addresses or
links contained in this book may have changed since publication and
may no longer be valid. The views expressed in this work are solely those
of the author and do not necessarily reflect the views of the publisher,
and the publisher hereby disclaims any responsibility for them.

The author of this book does not dispense medical advice or prescribe the use
of any technique as a form of treatment for physical, emotional, or medical
problems without the advice of a physician, either directly or indirectly. The
intent of the author is only to offer information of a general nature to help
you in your quest for emotional and spiritual well-being. In the event you use
any of the information in this book for yourself, which is your constitutional
right, the author and the publisher assume no responsibility for your actions.

Any people depicted in stock imagery provided by Thinkstock are models,
and such images are being used for illustrative purposes only.
Certain stock imagery © Thinkstock.

Print information available on the last page.

ISBN: 978-1-5043-6854-4 (sc)
ISBN: 978-1-5043-6855-1 (e)

Balboa Press rev. date: 11/09/2016

A Light in Our Life

Behold, I came into the world to be a light unto you, a light for the Jews and the Gentiles, a light to those who believe and to those who choose not so to do. A light for all, including you.

I will be a light unto your feet – a light to guide you along the righteous paths I have prepared for you.

Behold my children I am your God and King, I have chosen you from the beginning. Come close, come unto me, worship and give praise. I love you all, I love you deeply, always.

Walk worthy of the vocation wherewith I have called you. Behold you are my children, go boldly and in righteousness. Go in my love, go with my light.

Be gentle, my children, be gentle. Be gentle with my love as I am gentle with you, Show my gentle love to your friends and neighbours, show them the gifts I have given you, and go boldly in my love knowing all is well.

A Little Birdie Taught Me

A sassy little sparrow landed on the garden
gate. She chirped a cheery tune.
She was thankful for the sun of day and
that the night was lit by moon.

She expressed her thanks as she dashed here and there,
Her cheerfulness took away the darkness
which earlier had appeared.

With song and chipper movements she danced along the rail.
She was glad for family and for the rain that followed dusty days.

She appreciated the seeds which found their way to her domain.
With a chirp she kicked up her feet, blew
a kiss and went on her way.

Yep, that sparrow sure is wise.
And from this cheery bird I came to realize
That a song and thankfulness
Outshines the greyness of any skies.

A Loved One Is Missing

A loved one has died, and you feel bereft. Tears find their way across your cheeks and fall off your chin into that now soggy handkerchief. Your heart aches, worry awakes and you wonder how you will manage. I know, I've been there too.

Do not dismay nor be anxious. Your loved one is yet nearby, learning further lessons, experiencing a new realm. It is for just these reasons your loved one left heaven and arrived within the frame you knew, and who is yet nearby and thinks of you. It is not yet time for you to join them in this state, but that time will in due course arrive, so patiently await. They look forward to reunion soon.

Take time to listen for that voice, feel the love that's loud and clear, their spirit whispers even today, as knowing, rather than vibration of the air becomes your understanding that your loved one is well, in good hands, and very near.

Days will pass at Earth School while you learn the lessons you agreed upon, and one day when you are old enough you'll meet again in distant realm; meet, embrace, and hold one another close. And never part again.

A Response to a Request

A friend e-mailed asking for my prayers for two family members who were under the attack of cancer.

I pondered how I should respond, and as I did God reminded me that sometimes illness is to what appears as death, at other times it's for our growth.

God bless us all and lead us to the light. We acknowledge illness can be a path to redemption, and that it can lead us to truth.

We pray you will continue, ever near, whether we live in health or find ourselves heading to the other realms.

Sent, in love to you.

Abrasive Attitude and Actions

There are those who appear to walk through life with abrasive attitude and actions. Do not avoid these harmed individuals. Under apparent bravado is a heart yearning for the love and understanding which has never been provided.

Where possible, nod, agree and provide space for deliverance. Seek first a spiritual outcome which will honor all parties.

Let worries, dissatisfaction and anger simply evaporate. See how they are replaced by light, awe and new intentions.

Retribution and despair disappear, you feel lighter and look tranquil. This healthy alternative will cause you to live longer and more happily. Be love.

Always Loved

Years and years ago, when I was just a toddler, my dad let me step upon his toes and taught me how to dance. He took me and my siblings to the beach and taught us all to swim. He showed us love in many ways over many months and days, and taught us how to live.

As a family we watched the Lawrence Welk show and sang along to the hymns my sister Norah played upon a tired piano.

My mother was a mother bright, kind, thoughtful. Not only did she care for us she cared too for the community and was concerned about the wellbeing of neighbours as well as friends. Many a prayer left her heart for individuals, and for the world in general. Her soul ached for those who were in need and she tried to do what she could do to lessen hunger, worry, pain.

Her chewy molasses cookies were a welcome part of many a gathering and her warm thoughtful manner helped us all. Yes, there were times we'd have our differences, but I was always loved.

Norah: a precious sister and friend; always loved.

Ambassador

Come, Holy Spirit, I ask; teach me - that I might be an ambassador of truth, love and kindness.

Open my eyes to see as you see – righteousness unfolding, love prevailing, hearts cleansed and mankind serving others with grace and understanding.

Guide please, we ask, those of us who write, those of us who speak, and the many that witness your wisdom and grace.

Free our tongues to speak truth and hope, firm our backbones and our intentions so that we follow through as we ought with kindness and strength.

May we be instruments of light shining in a very real world as well as amongst the realms of angels and of glory. Amen

An Impression

The Lord, Jesus Christ, God Almighty is on his way. Because of this the wrath of the enemy is great and it makes every effort to disrupt homes, and lives. Stand firm on the truth – which is the word of God.

It would seem there is a spirit keeping God's word from spreading and yielding a harvest.

That spirit is *indifference.*

Lift me up Lord, and you my spiritual friends, be lifted up with me, I pray, with thanksgiving. Let's join together with like mind, watching for the coming of friend and savior.

Amen and Amen

Angels Enfold Me

We are surrounded by the angles of the Lord.
Their wings shield, their eyes are watchful,
Their arms are ready to catch a faltering step,
Or to embrace us in our loneliness.
Give thanks. Yes, Father, I do.
I praise you and offer you the incense of love.
My load is lightened with a song.
My strength sustained with gratitude.

Laughter and a merry heart
Coax gladness from those nearby. I will be forthright
and mindful of the hurt of others. I will bind, lift,
encourage. In doing so I too am healed, set free. Amen

Answered Prayer

Day after day the sun shone down upon our vibrant land. Trees turned brown and brittle. The land ached for a rainy day.

Here and there a careless operation, lightening or a wayward butt, set alight forests which succumbed to the flames in spite of valiant attempts to contain or to put them out.

Acre after acre cried as it was turned to ash and misery while pumps and lines of hose tried to douse the treacherous flames which ate our beautiful province.

Many of us sent prayers heavenward asking for a gift of rain. God heard our words, hastened t'ord us with drops of every size, and them in great abundance.

We breathed a sigh of gratefulness, and joined our hearts in thankfulness to God. And as we did I heard the grass, the green, the tiny critters join with us in song:

Halleluiah, halleluiah, thanks be to the one who is and was and evermore shall be, who listened to our call and graciously sent rains, rains which gave our land new hope. We give thanks, thanks from the bottom of our hearts.

Apologies, Father God

Apologies Father/Mother God for the delay. At this time your handmaiden listens.

You are not admonished but loved and cherished. We appreciate the family business you were about.

Difficult times are on the horizon but so are times of the overflowing of love and compassion, of measured kindnesses and what you might call 'the necessities of life.

Be alert. See who needs a cheerful smile or an encouraging word or a little cash put in their hand.

You have an abundant life, you have hope, love, and a compassionate heart. Continue in kindness.

Assuredly

In a bright blue sky a family of cream puff clouds suddenly appear, yet later as a breeze arrives they are no longer to be seen. I wonder... where have they gone?

Though they cannot now be seen with my human eyes, it is not that they are no more. For, assuredly, they maintain their essence, they simply continue in another form.

This continuity of being pertains not only to the water cycle, but to me and you and all. When death arrives, and takes us to another realm, fear not. As, assuredly, we maintain our essence, continuing on as soul. *Did you note owl and globes?*

Author Bio of Maureen

I did not set out to be an author. I was one seeking knowledge and an understanding of life. In my meditations I had conversations with energy I know as Spirit, whom I relate to as father/mother/sister/brother/cousin/friend and whom I call God.

In meditation I wrote down the words I heard, the thoughts that visited me. Sometimes I revisited earlier messages, as I found doing so strengthened me and gave me comfort. Notes here and there, and scraps of paper of various colours with numerous insights piled up. As a tidy person who likes order, I called out for help. "God", I asked, "what do I do with all of this?"

Knowing came upon me, it was clear, we had to make a book. And so *Inspired by God* was born.

And I say 'born' for a reason, it is not a quick and easy task. But it is significant, and worthwhile.

Well, that was the first book, *Still* followed and I started *Wisdom* – which is, at this writing, almost there. At about that time I had a request from God. Would I pen stories of the past lives I knew I'd had. As I'm probably the best person to do that, what could I say but 'Yes'? Maybe you will find *Life after Life after Life* on the shelves before long.

Avoid Wickedness

There's a lot of learning for us here on earth. Finding our
way through the labyrinth of life takes keen intent.

If we are not careful it's easy to slip off the righteous
trail. And hard, then, for wisdom to prevail.

But prevail we will for we know there is help at hand. We'll
converse with Source, sign up again, try a little harder and
from situations which mean 'trouble' we'll refrain.

God, you bless me with the wisdom I need,
and give me strength to embrace righteousness.
Thank you, that under your care I remain.

I join with a brother or sister who needs to be upheld,
together we are one, powerful and wise.
We will live in truth with no more greed or lies.
Amen

Balance

The inner you calls for balance, for
conversation, stillness, elation, exercise.
And enjoy the quiet - relish it a while.

Soon noise and worldly demands will
challenge the energy you set aside;
Energy which is needed to deal with the
turmoil which now arrives.

And, yet, you need that crazy pace, the laughter and confusion.
Be exuberant and thankful. Enjoy what comes your way.
Put worry on hold – at least for today.
Balance is preservation.

Be Centered

Develop first the power and grace which have been given. See then a world touched by the God you know – a touch which will enliven, delight, sustain.

Then you'll find your roots are centered; you will have strength for self and strengths to awaken in others.

You will be able to give and never know a decrease in love available to share or in light which will guide the way.

Look for it – the light shines on the path that you walk, and on the words that you shall share.

Be there.

Listen with your heart as well as with your ears.

Be ready to receive a message for the humble, encouragement for the poor and love for those who are lost and cannot find their way home.

Guide.

Be Still, Hearken unto the Voice of the Lord

Verily, verily. I say unto you, you shall enter my rest. Whoso would may enter. Come unto me and I will refresh you. I will give you living water, I will feed you with the bread of heaven.

To you, this day is given first, peace; second joy, third rest from worldliness. Come then with rejoicing before me for you are beloved. Honour me, look to me in all you do. Seek my face and you will find me.

Hearken yet unto the voice of God.

Come my child, come unto me for I love you. Lean on me and I will carry your burden. For all who would shall find their rest in me. Be ye yoked with me; together we will unfasten those things which should be loosed. We will tie together those which should be bound.

Yes, my child, know this – I am your Father who loves you. I am your mother will feed you and care for you. Feast at my table – for there you shall be comforted and fed and watered. You shall grow even as a plant grows. You shall blossom forth and not wither. Yea you shall blossom even as the cactus in the desert.

Change Occurred

In the oneness that exists a wondrous change
occurred, the one was split apart.
One became two - the yin and yang, good/evil,
order/chaos, discord/harmony, light/dark.

One had not dissolved, it was pure and clean, but
choice was now an issue and with it came responsibility,
culpability, and the concept of individuality.

We have the option of love/hate, righteousness/
dissident, unruly/patient,
in the challenges we find.
Still we can turn to doing what is right, good,
and of service to mankind.

As we ponder the path that we should
take, consider, give it attention…
For what we do, or do not do, is one thing, but more
important than the doing is our intention.

Charity

The lead story on today's 6 o'clock news might lead you to an act of charity, or you may be inclined to give a gift to one in need because some time ago another did the same for you, and though you may not be able to reciprocate to him or her, you choose to 'pay some forward'.

Be charitable too with leniency, kindness, benevolence and tolerance. Commit love to others and judge not. And when you give, give graciously with good intent – not thinking of the 'write off' you'll acquire or the buzz caused by your gift and formal attire.

What you do, and why you do it, are known to you and to the All-in-All; therefore be gracious, modest and thoughtful; for what you have done will, one day, return the call. May you be found with honorable choices.

Child You Are Mine

You are mine, I love you, and indeed I have
loved you from the beginning.
You have not chosen me, but I have chosen you
And I will keep you unto the end.

I have not called you to be an evangelist, but to be wife,
mother, husband, father, and through it all to show love.

The arm of flesh will fail you. Money isn't worth the cost.
Pray that the Lord will reveal His mighty right arm.

Look up. Trust me, your God, and lean
not to your own understanding.
I will make straight paths for your feet, I will guide you
and protect you as you walk along the paths I show you.

Love your neighbour, do good to those that
despise you. Overcome evil with good.
Pray for those in authority and for those
whom you would bless. For *I Am.*

I will place my words upon your lips and
my thoughts in your heart.
Forget not the underprivileged, those who cannot
repay in like manner. Remember I am with you
even unto the ends of the earth. Amen

Close

Lord God you are close. I feel your love, hear your thoughts, and write these words which you have wrought. These words are yours which we will share with others who need to know you care.

They need to know they are not alone, but that many route for them. For though she may seem 'gone', grandma, friend, or sister who wasn't here for long is now in Spirit with eternal wisdom at their side, they know one cannot die. The love continues,

But shame and hatred can be erased as we learn to live a faithful life in a thankful way. Amen

Come Into My Presence

God called me into His presence and we visited.

Meet with me and let me meet with thee. My salvation is for all who will receive it, it is not limited.

Ears will be unstopped, hearts opened and the message of salvation will be shared with a hungry, thirsting people.

The God you know shall be revealed in glory and in power to those who believe in my name. Seek for reality of God as the Father, the Son, and the Holy Spirit. "Who so ever will" is welcome, whosoever will" may come.

Step towards the Christ in faith; for have I not said "Draw nigh unto me and I shall draw nigh unto thee?" Even if it is a small, hesitant step that is taken, I still happily, and with love, meet with that person. So be it.

Come rest in me and share the love I place within your heart. I am your health, your strength, and you are the window through which my light can shine.

Lord I trust in you. Amen

Confirmation

Yes, you did listen to God, and you have changed your intentions – good. Keep up the good work...with righteous action or lack of action as the case may be.

The Father will give you strength,

Family and friends will encourage,

Mary herself will bless you with love and understanding.

Be cognizant of the many who gather with you in the spirit realm and in the time and space in which you presently dwell.

Recognize yourself as blessed.

I do. I will, and I give thanks.

Consolidate

Let the one you know as God fill your heart with love, and with the Holy Spirit.

Do not be a 'loner' but find others (there are many) who share your spiritual understandings.

There is strength in numbers; when others join you in similar thinking there is power. Power begets more power and strength; it acts as a magnet attracting others who, with you, benefit from consolidation of thought, consolidation of love. Become as one.

Darkness Had No Defense

Sunshine crept around the corner,
Bit its way through envy and despair.
It made a place where light could reappear.

Darkness had no defense,
It couldn't override the gladness and the
happy hearts
Which appeared from nowhere.

Light had done it again,
It saw the change of heart it had provided
And the optimism that decided
To join in the display of joy and well-being.

De-escalate

Our tone, our eyes, the volume of our speech should be under
spiritual control if we wish to de-escalate a tense situation.

Allow the strength of Spirit to give us ears to hear the
cry, the fear that is hidden in a desperate soul.

Maintain equilibrium and allow Godly wisdom
an opportunity to address with right and carefully
filtered words, the thoughts we share.

Remember then to give thanks where thanks is due. Make
a mental note of what worked or of what did not. Amen

Slow and steady Iceberg finds her way to the sea.

Dispute

Think carefully before you choose to dispute.
What is the most important thing you can
do, or show, or know at this time?

The world is before you with some upheaval,
some pain, but also with much peace.
Calm dispute, encourage love and forbearance.

If we meet up with things that give us fear, what can we learn,
what can we teach, what improvements can take us higher?

Drawer of Love

I have opened the door of love.
I scoop up armfuls which I scatter with abandon.
I see it seep into the souls of me and many.

I open the door of cleanliness, I am washed in
the blood of the lamb. Every spot is clean, every
wrinkle dissolved. Every blemish is gone.
All my hurts abated, not because I deserved it,
But, simply, because God provides it, I accept it.

Drawer of Blessings

Blessed are those whose intention is to harm not,
but to lift, encourage and admonish.

Blessed are those whose tears fall for the plight of others and
who do not stop at tears, but also loosen their purse strings.

Blessed are the tender hearted for they comfort many.
Blessed are the wise for they will not be swallowed by greed.
Blessed are the generous – they reap what they sow.

Blessed are the gentle, they will bind the wounded,
encourage the downhearted. As they do it will be done
to them. Blessed are the hungry who share even their
meager supplies. They will sit at a table of plenty.

Dressing Up

Now and again I get dressed up and I need a place to go.

Sometimes I need a place to go but determine dressing
up is not in vogue – as likely we both know.

I want to look the part I 'play' yet I want to play
from depths within, from heart and soul.

I'd like to show in all I do that I respect the land in which I
dwell, and Mother/Father God and Christ that I love you.

I expect that you and I can be a blessing to our
globe, a blessing to the lives which here unfold.

We'll not be stingy nor greedy - wanting our own way, but
wanting instead fairness for those who hold us close.

God, you bless and please us. Restore, we ask, our
hearts with love and thankfulness. Amen

Dwell in Kindness

One by one, and in groups of two or three
Spirit houses in the frames we be.
Our bodies become the home of divinity
As the goodness of God settles in me and in thee
And in all who welcome a holy eternity.

Love one another.
Dwell in kindness and thoughtfulness,
Be joyful in your work or play;
Learn what you must on this earthly stay.
And take care of Earth, she's a fragile globe
Who needs our input and needs our love.
She'll provide for us (within limits)
But is challenged by avarice and carelessness.

God, help us we pray,
To dwell in kindness to the land, the sea,
The air we breathe, the plants, the creatures
And all who need our love and not our greed.

Embrace Love

Examine the world in which you dwell and the skies which have a story to tell. See the order, the majesty, and the oneness of eternity.

Become at one with love and kindness, of all that is and all that was. Embrace the love within, the love without and all around, let that light and love surround us all.

Encouragement Requested

I want to walk in a godly way,
And choose a righteous home.
So, Lord, I ask for encouragement
And holy choices of my own.

I choose to listen to your gentle voice
And watch for your directions,
I'll heed the visions you design
And work with your intentions.

When impatience raises is dreadful head
Help me, I pray to calm my soul
And act as you would lead.

Amen

Evolution

Even on our worst days we are evolving,
Probably evolving faster than we would if
everything fell in harmony onto our plate.

Everything happens for a purpose, and the purpose
may be to brighten the light you are.

Shine. Allow the glow of life, the effervescence of
hope be a beacon to those seeking wisdom.

Faith, Hope and Happiness

We are those who can bring faith, hope and happiness to the discouraged and downhearted.

There are many who are lost in a dark place who look for even a glimmer of light to give them direction. Yet we have, within, a flame – a light which never dies. We will attract those who seek, search, ponder.

Let us be honest, forgiving. We will be a conduit of understanding and knowledge, for few know, as do we, that life is eternal. There are generations ahead and behind us. We will continue learning, teaching, blessing. Let us bend to love, undo the pain we've caused, or the pain we have endured.

We chart a new map, one which does not wander into materialism, greed or avarice. Let us use that map to take us into regions where we can be of service to those who ask for sustenance of body, mind or soul.

Know it is by grace we find ourselves in a position which allows us to be generous and kind. Therefore sow seeds of comfort, kindness, hope and give thanks that we can so do.

Father/Mother God

May my intentions meet with your hopes for me?
May I be in a place to which you'd agree?
For Father/Mother God, I want to work with thee.

So, when you see that I'm off track
Please open my eyes and bring me back.
For I'd rather be where you'd have me be
In a place of love and integrity.

Few Find

Many there be who seek, but few find.

And why is this?

Ah... they seek that which is useless – Honour, Riches, Fame.

Let us approach with humble hearts, and a mind which yearns for truth. Then we will be met along a path which leads us to the wisdom we can put to good use, and the kindness we'll apply.

Let's open our heart, see it blossom and give forth a sweet perfume which will heal, encourage and uplift. No corner will be left untouched. We will be provided with the energies needed, the breath of life and the falling away of stupidity.

Thank you Holy Spirit, we look to you.

Forgetfulness

Once you have learned from the awkward situations that may clasp you, throw the residue into the sea of forgetfulness. Do not harbour grudges or keep returning to examine the experience; instead look in a new direction, look to hope, courage, friendship. Look to light, peace, joy. See wisdom take the place of retaliation, abundance replace paucity.

Acknowledge the kingdom of God within and give Spirit opportunity to dissolve regrets ad replace them with understanding. Then give thanks, help the poor, absolve yourself of negative encumbrances.

Spirit is here with encouragement. Listen, as you do. Speak softly as is your want. You will be provided with wisdom to share, healings for anxious hearts, and the opening of eyes to an abundant life of what really matters.

So be it Father/Mother God.

Frank Approach

We 'beat around the bush' not knowing what to say or do; not wanting to commit to, or close, the decisions that must be made. Procrastination helps awhile, diversions do their best, but without a kindly solution I can't sleep upon my bed, can you?

How about a frank approach spoken with gentle tone? How about honesty in what we've done or left undone? How about a plan for future clarity in conversation?

And let's have a plan to heal the hurt and pain which blew up in this altercation. Admit, apologize. Agree to make changes that will benefit the parties as required. Then proceed to undo wrong and chart a course where love can lead.

May this ever be - for thee and me also, if you so please.

Free from Fear

I choose to free self from fear. I can do this, Christ, because you have given me courage.

I will not worry about my end of life, for I know the final judgement will be a 'final healing' with a right evaluation. I will know what is worthy, what is not. I will want to keep only that which is good, the other creations will no longer exist. When everything I retain is 'loveable' there is no reason for fear to remain in me.

'Knowing' with certainty is knowledge, it is beyond time, it is of the one I know as God. Knowledge can always be remembered as it has never been destroyed - being, as it is, a matter of Spirit.

My mind will be reunited with the mind of Christ, for I ask you Spirit to erase errors and misconceptions from my mind. Be, please, my guide.

All are called but few choose to listen. I choose to listen in peace, and in God's rest; may I dwell in the peace which allows this.

Free or Freedom?

There is a cost to everything; the death of a soldier, likely the death of many soldiers, for a country's freedom, the price of an unhealthy environment to accommodate a weed-free acreage of wheat, or the cost of the extra calories in that 'free' treat.

Beware of 'free' as it often adds to poor choices. Look instead for freedom; freedom to choose the gracious and kind manor of speech which Spirit can provide. Or to choose freedom to be the thoughtful, generous person that lives within your skin.

Accept freedom to live within the walls of hope, love and your budget – be clothed with grace and happiness. These are more significant than anything which money might acquire.

In peace I lay my head upon my pillow. In peace I close my eyes and whisper prayers. In peace, and with gratitude I rise in the morning seeking to do God's will. Amen

From the 'Pulpit'

As Debbie said last Sunday,
"In life we have to live, we have to work, to put a
roof over our heads, and food on the table.
But life doesn't end there."

So true; may we see the bigger picture.

There is also a spiritual side to life that must be
lived. We are responsible for self – no excuses.
It's up to us to do what we know is good, is right,
And to do it in a way that we are able.

The joys and challenges we've been through
have made us who we are and who we yet will
be. In the days ahead, let us learn, be of service
and reach out to those who seek us.

Getting Closer

I want to get closer to you Father God. I want to know your will and do your bidding knowing you will not take from me free will or opportunity to chart my own path.

I am aware that the Spirit of God knows our wishes and gives us signals. Let's be receptive to the urgings of our heart. Let's learn the importance of being still with quiet mind. Let information come to self as if it arrives telepathically. Let it 'pop' into our heads, our soul.

We will not flaunt our abilities, nor claim fame from them. We will keep kindness and gentle truth in mind as we share the gift of God chosen words. We'll treat all we meet, all we know, with unconditional love.

Glimmer of Light

Fog crept into my heart and soul, it darkened my thoughts, distracted me from the pathway of light on which I had walked. For a time I ignored it and just kept keeping on.

One fortuitous day I realized I needed to seek a glimmer of light, for I knew that even a glimmer of light would get me started on the road to recovery. It took some looking, it took 'tasting' and spitting out. It took guts and focus to leave the darkness and hang on to the small stretch of light I found.

As I changed my speech to echo with positive intent, and as I put negative impressions immediately into the trash bin when they arrived, and looked instead at the small streak of light with hope, the glimmer grew, grew again until there soon was no place where it was not. Skies were still grey, yes, associates disgruntled, true, and family earnest with their own concerns; but spiritual light followed me and lit my path.

You are wished the same; let's stand firm in our agreement that goodness will both follow us and also point the way; that the great and holy Spirit, which we may know as God, will keep always a light lit which we may follow with joy and gladness.

Go with Light and Wisdom

Behold, you will be surrounded by light and wisdom. Go with it. Hesitate not. Add a note or two, hear the song that hides within the prose.

Lift your eyes to the hills. Bless the rain that cleanses all who, like you, are touched by it. Look up see heaven opened, see the stars bring forth their songs. Sing along with them once more. Be drenched with heavenly energy, let it settle in your soul. Look for understanding, seek the path you ought to follow. The path is there, and there is more to claim.

God I don't know where I'm going, but with your guidance I go there just the same.

Protect me, please, and those who seek to do your will, keep us from wrong doing, pick us up, please, when we fall.

God Sustains Me

I cease worrying about what may happen to me.
I put each day in God's hands, disavowing the
inner turmoil which tries to crowd me.

As it arrives, I turn each day over to the one I know as God,
welcoming things as they are - without reservation.

I keep moving forward. Even if I feel alone, I know the
love that lifts me and keeps me on the right path. Today,
once more, I find my greatest strength – faith.

I am held in the cupped hands of God.

Good, Honest, Holy, Beautiful

I am to create good and that which is honest, beautiful, holy. I chose to fulfill the will of God. Heart to heart, spirit to spirit, will I relate to my brothers and sisters, my cousins and friends Though it will seem for a time that I am fulfilling this physically - in a body as it were - it will be with perception and vision that I will work.
I will relegate distortions of wisdom to ash and watch as the ash is blown away.

Lord, your ability to create is with me; it has always been thus. I desire to extend this creativity through me to others who desire it too. I am not separated from God but am at one with him/her. Lord awaken me, quicken my spirit and let a fresh anointing fall on me, and not on me only but on others who claim it too. Thank you

Stand strong for that which will help mankind in the long run, continue to grow, be a peacemaker in the day you experience as 'today'.

At different times of the year, trees wear glorious colours. They know their time and place in the story of autumn. Some, content, continue on in their greenery. May we have similar wisdom, knowing when changes are in order, or when we should rest in the cloak that covers us.

Good Intensions

I'm glad my God is gracious, long suffering, holy, kind.
For even if I botch it up
My good intentions help me find
Relief, love, long suffering and joy.

Join with me in laughter, in gentleness and love.
Let's be discreet
but just the same
Make a happy difference to those we meet.

Let's do our best where we find ourselves
Not expecting reward or praise.
Then we'll find our spiritual debts, taxes and all,
are paid.

Some years ago my second husband received a diagnosis of prostate cancer. Even though he had been through treatments and was given hope he seemed to know his time was short. He made adjustments to his life and set in order what he could. One day he told me he was receiving visits from an elderly couple who had cared for him when he was a child, and one morning he told me a strange short little guy had met him in his dreams. He told me that this 'leprechaun' visited, said his sins had been paid in full, even the taxes. And so it was. This writing is in remembrance of Arthur – a wonderful man, a wonderful husband.

Good Morning
A Visitor Arrived with a few words:

Good morning, it's a pleasure to be among you. I am Spirit here to teach you about the world. I once lived here, have recently learned new lessons. I am no wiser than you – we all have desire to learn and grow. We also have restlessness which drives our soul forward.

When men fall apart, mankind falls apart, loses links
with one another – this often brings about war. Let us see
from another's view, make allowances, and include.

Though all stood for freedom, life went wrong. Many have
died – see the monuments. You are blessed who have not
been called to fight. Be a peace maker in the days you have,
and today is one of those. Be a friend – that is soul at work.
Stay away from situations which will bring harm to others.

What purpose is at hand for us? Hard work, a striving for
goodness, for perfection. Change self. Look into the mirror
to see where there is room for improvement. All around you
is everything you need, and within is the drive to do your
best, to set a good example. Let it be so, and so it will be.

Earth is like a heaven; when you get there you
will see that you can continue to grow.

Be a peacemaker – today. Avoid rancor and abuse. Be
willing to change self. Look in a mirror and see where there
is room for improvement. All around you is everyone you
need, and all you need to know and do. There is no end
to the opportunities for growth and Godly learning.

Stand strong for that which will help mankind in
the long run, continue to grow, be a peacemaker
in the day you experience as 'today'.

At different times of the year, trees wear glorious colours.
They know their time and place in the story of autumn.
Some, content, continue on in their greenery. May we
have similar wisdom, knowing when changes are in order,
or when we should rest in the cloak that covers us.

Hand in Hand with God

Would you go a walking, a walking
Hand in hand with the Holy Spirit, with the God that you know?
Would you clean your speech, your thoughts and your intent?

Would you trade riches for tender hearts nearby,
And wait upon the outcome
Without asking 'When? Or Why?

Could you look upon a cloudy sky
Or cranky situation
And know all is in the hands
of an everlasting love who knows your mind, who helps you find
the peace for which you pray today?

May this be so for each of us
Who choose to walk hand in hand
With the love we know as Mother/Father God.

And may that love bless us all
As we reach out and bless in kind.

Harmony

For harmony we need differences that work together,
where blending instruments and voices make more of
sound and life than could be done by any one of them.

When energies connect, merge and resonate, it
is not the individualities which please, but the
complexity of togetherness. Two tickets, please.

Let's roll this thought away from song and roll it
right on home. We too can work and play within
this frame, bringing love, receiving harmony.

Healthy Living

We are careful about what we eat and what we drink.
Let's learn to be careful about what we say, what we think.
There are vitamins in green veggies – they're a good choice.
Take note – there is power in your thought and in your voice.
Explore gratitude and peace of mind.
Practice thoughtfulness.
Find opportunities to be kind.
We are in process of becoming the best being we can be.
That may include exercise of the body and of possibility.

Hear This

Tomorrow is a new day.
You know you've made a mess of today.
Yes, you have.
You said what you ought not to have said,
You sulked, spoke aggressively and definitely scowled.
And now you feel terrible.
You know you 'blew it'.

You can think of no way to make amends,
And you are right, there is no way to recall yesterday.
Learn the lesson.
Learn to clamp your mouth shut when you feel so disagreeable.
Apologize.

Tomorrow is a new day. You can do better, you will do better.
Be gentle with yourself and with those who refuge with you.
Give everyone time and space to change and to refine their lives.
Do as you would have others do to you.
Amen

Heaven's Song

Do not be a harsh note in the song heaven weaves. Be instead the harmony, the sound instead which pleases.

Be the song of love, forgiveness and laughter. Be the kindness your globe needs.

Angels watch over you, your guides are close, 'tis true. They bring wisdom and understanding your way. Do then as you ought to do and give thanks.

For you are loved by many – some here on your plane, but many others in spirit claim responsibility and provide clever intervention. They help you find your way through the labyrinth your life has become.

'Ho Manna Hi'
My Spirit Waits on God

Spirit waits today on you, my God. My strength, my understanding comes from you. I fasten love to my heart, discrimination to my eyes, my ears. My tongue speaks only good and righteously.

Meanness is hidden, buried deep within the globe. Anger is dismissed, frustration put on hold. Spirit is invited to an honorable role.

What is this role?

Teach wisdom, teach kindnesses and love; then let it all fall into place. Live it. We are asked only to do our best, and that is what we do.

Some heed when they are called, some choose to join the actions of faith, some hurry away from the light. That is the choice of each; there is no coercion. We determine what we'll do and what we'll say. Let us help provide a way that all might make an informed decision.

It is not lost on me Father/Mother/Sister/Brother/Cousin/Friend that today you had me write in pen.

Honor *All that Is*

One thing I have learned is that there's no fooling God. God knows it all, is it all.

Honor *All that Is*, honor the God you know. Abandon thanklessness, blend with a more heavenly flow. Don't try to rush the rain, nor block the winds that blow. Be patient with yourself, you've come a long way, and there's still a way to go.

In some hearts faith is fragile, easily disrupted, but our will can bring it close where its power never ends. Let's wrap ourselves in faith, share it with our brothers, sisters, friends.

There's a lot for us to learn, and still a lot for us to do. Let's join with others who are 'up for it' too.

Be a peacemaker – today. Avoid rancor and abuse. Be willing to change self. Look in a mirror and see where there is room for improvement.

All around you is everyone you need, and all you need to know and grow. There is no end to the opportunities for growth and Godly learning. Do what you can do to make this globe a happier safer place.

Stand strong for that which will help mankind in the long run, continue to grow, be a peacemaker in the day you experience as 'today'.

At different times of the year, trees wear glorious colours. They know their time and place in the story of autumn. Some, content, continue on in their greenery.

May we have similar wisdom, knowing when changes are in order, or when we should rest in the cloak that covers us.

Am I One?

Am I one? Or am I two, or more?

This body that I live in seems to have desires of its
own, and mind has its own wishes too. Soul oversees
the pulls and pushes and attempts to lead the way.

Sometimes *truth* wins, sometimes, *lies*. Sometimes *heaven*
seems to own me, but at other times I'm in a *different guise*.

And there's a tugging that tries to lead astray.
But there's also a claim for wisdom at this time.

Holy spirit, friend of mine, I ask for guidance,
for 'common sense', and wise discussion. Amen

1

2

3

I Hear from God

Many days I hear from God.
Today is one of those.
I know I'm loved and cherished
I feel Spirit draw me close.

These days I hold within my soul
Wisdom and the flame of life, the fire.
For they lift and challenge me,
Feed me understandings I desire.

You can claim them too,
If wisdom is what you'd gather.
Look, search, have godly intent
And a heart that delivers service to others.

Spirit is nearby in me, in thee,
And in the movement of the tide, the stars,
the sea.

Together we believe that a gracious plan
Enfolds you, holds you, just as you are.
Then takes you where you want to be.

Amen

Improvement

Improving self takes will and inclination. It is a fair goal for which to aim. Things which seem hard at first become easier. You point yourself in the right direction and use the strength you have to walk the Godly journey you have chosen. Ah. It gets easier day by day, and actually fun.

Spirit does not judge you, but gives kudos. You were hit with turmoil in your personal life. You were brought low when world matters were amiss. But you let things in your own life fall into place, and gave thanks for the small steps of Earthly improvement that seemed to appear in the weekly news.

Be keen to help those you meet reach harmony. Put forward your kind thoughts, ask for wisdom in knowing what is not working, what should be abandoned. Listen to the quiet within who has answers, who will help you advance peace, kindness, love, goodwill and hope. With others join in ways which clean the environment, gladden the heart, and install right thinking, right living. A pebble dropped in a pond sends waves of energy which reach the distant shore. The 'little' that you choose to do can have far reaching consequence for one by one the waves bring light, and that is what you too will do. Love self, love others, and love this precious globe.

In the Presence of the Lord

I will walk forth in the presence of my Lord. Yes, in the presence of God there is joy forever more. There is wisdom and understanding in God's word. Oh my soul, rejoice and be glad.

These things are written for you who believe: speak kindly, speak softly both to your own, and to the world in general. Be gentle and loving clothed in my lovingkindness for I love you, I adore you, I cherish you. Behold you are in the very kingdom of God. Christ dwells within you.

Do not fret about what your work for God must be. Put even the Lord first, minister unto me in partnership and I will bring about ways for you to minister unto me even as you care for my little ones and for the people I shall bring into your life.

Find time to be quiet before me, listen to the voice of the Spirit of God. Feed upon the Word of God, dwell in it and God will dwell in you.

Intertwined

In this era we rush back and forth, protecting our
'own' space, possibly infringing on another's.

Is it time for us to see all space as one?
Is the globe a place where all may roam?

Should we contemplate a different plan where
there are no borders, no hazards, no fear?

Be centered – knowing from whence you come.
You are from the stars; the heavens you look to were your home.

Intertwine. Bend. Lend a hand. See self whole
when it works together or alone.

You rode the dust of enterprise to this plane,
And here you are on the globe you claimed.

Be generous and kind - regarding Earth anew; it's
a home away from the home you knew.

You're on an adventure with experiences which help
you grow. Learn, and show others the way.

Sift righteousness from the common melee,
Keep the good, throw the dross away.

Intervention

Another difficult day, overwhelmed with extreme expectation from family as well as from a contractor working on the property. Ow!

God, I ask for grace to be able to speak softly and with wisdom. I do not want to make a fool of myself, nor do I wish to press those who are antsy already into an uncompromising corner.

I lay down my individuality and see self as part of all. Wisdom descends and we discuss the situation seeking a fair undertaking for us all. And so it is.

We are pleased to keep dealing with this team, and they give us a smile and 'high-five' as we part ways. We are all 'happy campers'.

Thank you Spirit of God, thank you for your intervention.

Invitation
Join Me as We Write!

These days many of us are listening to the still, quiet, spiritual voice which whispers to us.

We are blessed, encouraged, given hope and, yes, sometimes reprimand. We scribble the thoughts that are given to us in a booklet or add them to the ever expanding collection of bits of paper which have been used here and there at a moment's notice. One day we recognise that these gems of philosophy and spiritual insight are not for us alone. We'd like to share them. Is that you? Could it be you? Would you like to join me in my next book? Spirit has been encouraging me to make dedicated sections in my next book for dedicated authors. This way the wisdom you have gleaned is available for all. I have also been encouraged to share with you some learnings from an interesting book, which we can apply to our endeavor.

(Often I am given words which I cannot spell nor would have thought about); when I look them up I see they are perfect. Pays to listen.

Links: maureenmillar@shaw.ca Phone: 604 534 2635 I attach, *Writing Tips*, am open to comments. Contact me if you have questions or writings you'd like to share. Maureen

It Was Christmastime

Mostly I go along with the illusion of time. I set my alarm if I have to meet friends or keep an appointment. I boil the eggs for 6 minutes, bake the cookies for twenty. However in the reality I also embrace, I know there is no time, there is only 'now'. The so-called 'dead' are lively in their chosen realm; they're open to conversation, exchange of thought, reparation.

Spirit entities abound, they're often around me watching thoughtfully. They help me find lost items, correct my English, add to its form. I'm never alone; some are so close I wonder how much privacy I don't have!

Recently my mom, dad, a brother and a sister (who have all passed) arrived for a visit, together!

It was wonderful to have their visit and I was especially happy the four of them had connected for the Christmas season was upon us; this brought our fond remembrances into focus.

These four are dearly loved as are many others who for one reason or another left this plane and headed for another. They've met with friends, are learning and may teach, understand our yearnings, want us to know they are in reach. Speak to them and smile, hangout for a while, accept the love and wisdom that they bring. Amen

Writing Tips

Because of my personal interest in Atlantis, I picked up a book –
**The Sea Gods after Atlantis - The Biography of a Race of
Man.** (By Valerie Bonwick and Jonathan Bigras) In amongst the
curious tales and considerations was a section about Telepathy and
Conservation of Verbal Energy which included material I found
pertinent. Following are the notes I took from *The Sea Gods after
Atlantis,* enjoy.

Hot air is for balloons not for spiritual correspondents.

Concentrate writings rather than being long winded. Utilize
energy rather than wasting it on something which would not be
encouraging, good, kind.

Think before you write, even as you think before you speak.
Sustain thought. Choose words wisely. Construct an image which
is visually perfect. Listen with all your intention to whatever is
being communicated to you.

Take notes, but suspend your response until there is a break in the
incoming transmission. Remember, it is always a mark of poor
self-control to interrupt. Experience joy within, delve into the
experience. Acquire self-discipline – it is regarded as a social grace.
Communicate precisely and accurately.

Join Me

Decades ago, before it was taboo, I walked in Stonehenge.
I was overwhelmed by the size, the solitude,
the energy that dwelt there.

I realized God was there and walked with me too.
"I have walked where God has been."

That understanding followed me home.

As heavy rains fell and the wind howled I
became aware of my lack of humanity.
I knew I must seek and find an answer to that frailty.

Father/Mother/God I seek grace and
kindnesses which will take me there.

Reader…come.
Join me if you care.

Joy

A loved one arrives. Spontaneously you put the kettle on and reach for treats. You embrace and smile. Your heart is light, laughter comes easily; the air is filled with joy in the exchange of cheerful chatter.

This is time well spent; see how it lifts you and energizes your spirit and the spirit of your visitors.

Allow the sacred energy of love which dwells within to brush lightly the hearts and hopes of those nearby. Let it sink deeply into soul.

Experience again thoughtfulness and honest smiles.

Find joy in a job well done, in the success of determination, and the gentle flow of genuine conversation.

Find joy in the upturned lips of a special friend, the knowing look of that special someone, or the exuberance of a welcoming hug.

A Kinder Globe

Join me as I imagine a softer, kinder globe,
One where love, laughter and an inner glow
Begins shining in us all.

A world where grudges are erased,
And worries are replaced with love
Or at the very least with tolerance.

Let's begin with understanding;
For we have walked only in our own shoes,
And sometimes poorly at even that.

Cloak self with compassion.
Be there for those who seek us out,
For they see in us what they want to be.

Bless those who come your way,
For those who would benefit, it is time well spent
Lend a hand, or an ear, faith, hope, good cheer,

For one you can help has arrived.
We need not go 'a hunting'.
We'll welcome instead those who come within our space.
We'll meet with those who seek the light
Joining them in love and grace.

Principles from Deuteronomy

We are ordinary people living in a time which is anything but ordinary. There is a new experience before us. Let's learn from negative experiences of the past and from hope within our soul.

We've been at this stage of evolution long enough. Be ready to be part of something new.

The world is before us; this is the land of the Lord which is to be shared anew. Form groups which will be accountable to one another and to the Devine. Choose overseers who are wise, who are impartial in the decisions they will have to make. Do not be afraid nor discouraged.

The God you know has brought you this far; part of the journey lies ahead but there is no rush. Follow the timing appointed, heed the still voice of Spirit.

Keep to your own tasks. Do not get involved in issues which are not on your agenda. Problems which seem too overpowering are no more difficult to overcome than the least of encumbrances. Stand. Fail not.

There is enough for all. Dismiss the concept of poverty. Put the concept of being disenfranchised behind you. Expect to see the glory of God; you have seen this before, and will see it again.

Focus on the one you know as God, as Spirit as the All in One, the Almighty.

Run not in various directions seeking first this teaching, then 'that. The God you know watches over you; pay attention to directives.

Ageless

Some who appear to be old are young is Spirit. Some whose years are few are burdened, bent with cares. Be joyful in knowing the shell may age but Spirit is eternal.

You are indeed ageless but be mindful of timelessness even as you appear to dwell in time.

And be aware of 'heaven' even as you dwell on Earth. What you see with your eyes will one day be no more for even the sky and all the stars shall be rolled up and set aside. What you see with spiritual vision is as eternal as the love of a mother for her little one.

Lessons from the Sea

Isn't it amazing how the sea can receive or give?

How its form finds a home where all is one, where
many creatures live and in this oneness thrive!

Consider, too, the oneness of being born
into a place where all are connected
whether enormous whale,
some version of a fish,
or a worm that swims and squirms.

I can see there's a lot for me to learn!

Let us Look Up

Verily, verily, I say unto you, look up. For yet a little while and you shall see me. You shall see me in glory and power with hosts praising my new name. I come in strength, my joy complete.

Yet a little while and a time of great darkness shall be on the face of the earth, but be not dismayed for it must be that scripture is fulfilled. And after yet a little time unto thee shall the Son of man appear as a fiery dart with the sound of trumpet and with hosts proclaiming his glory.

Holy Spirit teach thou me to look for the return of my Savior with gladness and hope, for their will be great joy at his coming. Praise God, praise God, Alleluia the anthem rings. Unto us has the child of Bethlehem become King indeed.

Behold I am with you even until the ends of the Earth. I am the light of a dark world. As it becomes darker you shall shine more brightly. Christ is in you, you are a light in a dark world.

Let Wisdom be Magnified

Ah, the depths that we might find in the massive rocks which curl together in form and spirit. Be blessed by the power found in them; that power signifies a 'flame' of energy, of power, and of a cleansing. Let the dross of life be burned to dust, the wisdom magnified.

Let memories be set right, let them be cut and polished with age. Know that with the knowledge gained in this 'go-round' as well as learning from the past, we have been left smarter, kinder and full of love.

The past, our past, brings strength and wisdom closer, solidly planted in all that is and all that is to be. Examine the flow of life, the yin, the yang. See what is shallow and of little use as opposed to that which is stalwart, firm, and worthy of your consideration.

Let's Do Our Best

Did you sing a song to God today?
Did you wish all well?
Did you lift the fallen, feed the hungry, and let wisdom prevail?

We are to do our best within the frame we find ourselves.
The lame are not expected to run a mile, or the
poor of heart to turn up with a smile.

But all of us are expected to do our best within the
structure we find ourselves. This is an individual
matter, all can serve one way or another.

Do what you know will please the Holy
One who shows you a holy way.
In time you are recompensed fairly, discreetly, and in kind.

For what you give with godly grace is what
you'll see bestowed, or visa versa.

May our eyes be opened to the good we can share, may
our intentions be, always, kind, loving and fair.

Let's Really Live

Hi, God, I'm here. It's me!
I'm prepped, and willing to really live, to learn,
to teach, to revel in this glorious moment.

Forgive me if I laugh too loudly,
Cry spontaneously, or seek a hideaway where I can regroup.

For what I see is fun, frolic, empathy and care.
But also there is sadness and an aching – everywhere.

Many know not that they are loved, accepted, cherished. They feel
left out, ignored, exploited. What do I say to these? "Believe"?

Kindness does not rise in every corner; in some greed and avarice
outweigh love - that's an option in the freedom we receive.

We have freedom to make choices; we aren't
living in a state of 'puppetry'.

"Do your best" – that's where it's at. Don't expect perfection
here today, yet see it making waves which come your way.

Life as a Fly

Recently, in a spiritual exercise, I found myself struggling to get out of a film that encased me. (It's not easy making an appearance when you've been squished in a small and sticky place.) I stretched. I stretched some more. Soon I tore the film which held me.

Once out I knew I was a maggot. I'd been sent on a mission, a mission of nature.

Ah, what lovely odors surrounded me, what tasty morsels enticed my hungry frame. I hunkered down at the compost pile and hung out there for a while. I grew, grew some more. My body changed, it took me awhile to learn how to move about with a modicum of grace – grace that I really worked at attaining as I'd spotted a potential partner who had divine eyes and a winsome way.

But she wasn't impressed with me – it was easy to see that :(

I must admit I pouted a bit and wondered what to do.

Imagine my surprise when I opened my eyes a few days later to find I had a bright green chin and sparkling wings which everyone adored. Incredibly one of the maggots came a little closer.

She needed help in getting out of her casing. I encouraged her in her strugglings, and soon she was set free.

And then when I found those pizza tidbits and offered them to her – she glowed and looked at me with a look I'd expect of a princess. How nice was that? We romped about, enjoyed the day and did what nature decreed.

Next day I crept upstairs to see if I could find a tasty morsel for my mate – my friend.

Then 'whack' and all things changed.

I lifted from the earth (as spirit) to see a gruesome splotch. That was me, I supposed. But I didn't fret. I'd done what I had come to do, and now, perhaps, I could head out on another interesting life.

Life or Death Conundrum

"Relax. Relax. It's not a life or death matter", we may hear as a friend encourages calmness or a rethinking of options which are apparent.

And how very true this saying is for there is only life, there is no death – just learning opportunities and a sendoff on to a new adventure.

Our job is to learn how to really live, to fully experience the days spent in Earth School. See these experiences enlarge your wisdom, and provide a way for you to become the magnificent being you are and whom you notice you are yet becoming.

You grasp the truth of an everlasting self and of that self making more of what is offered. We acknowledge the truth that there is no such thing as 'time', on the other hand we know it's time to really live!

Ah ha. Here comes wisdom!

Light from the Lighthouse

I was at an event the other day. Many appeared and seats were few. However there was no greed, no battling for choice places.

It was amazing. There wasn't a frown or a careless comment from anyone. I saw people at their best.

Hours later everyone left feeling, I believe, as good as I did - for what we had observed and experienced was love in action No crankiness, just loving interaction.

Thank you everyone who made this happen, and greetings as well to our friends in heaven.

The Light of the World

I am the Light of the world, the true light who makes light to shine in dark corners. I am Spirit, I am the Father who makes the light shine in you, who loves you and wants what is best for you.

There are many dark corners, but I, the true Light of the world shall reveal the evil intents of man's hearts.

Iniquity is rampant, the imaginings of man's heart and mind is vile, a thing of reproach to me. The father cannot look on those whose desires are evil.

Oh Lord that your lightness would reveal your goodness to them so that they would turn from sinful, selfish ways, and would follow you. Amen

Light-up Lives

Start by being satisfied with your life the way it is. It is like this for a reason, it is like this for a season of growth and examination.

You have been blessed and you are a blessing to others.
Fear not, nor fret. You are where you ought to be,
you are a beacon to another soul, a pilgrim who can
show the path where another may safely walk.

Like a Rock?

I dressed quickly and gathered together the items I'd need for a short trip to Vancouver Island. I would be on the ferry for a couple of hours there, and a couple more going back. Taking something to read seemed in order so I dashed over to a book cubby in the front room.

An interesting assortment of reading material met my eyes; but one book in particular, which had been passed on by a friend, caught my attention. It was large, chunky. When I ruffled though the pages I found it had well over five hundred pages. Just the ticket! I grabbed it and my bulging handbag and was soon aboard a British Columbia ferry - the *Queen of Alberni*. From its generous windows were amazing views of an unsettled sea edged by stalwart green trees which were in turn haunted by eagles, hawks, gulls galore and sometimes the call of ravens. It was like a mini cruise taking the ferry – the food was excellent and varied, the staff helpful, and it was easy to find treasures for self or loved ones in amongst the clothing and gift offerings. Interesting people, friendly chatter rounded out the day

Once I was settled I took a closer look at the chubby tome. My eyebrows lifted as I read the title: *The Convoluted Universe Book 4*.

Written, I noticed, by a Dolores Cannon, whoever she was. (I find she has written volumes of interesting material!)

Book 4! I wondered if there was any point in starting at 'Book 4'. Wouldn't the stage have been set and the characters developed in Books 1, 2 and 3? Was there any point? But as my options were limited, to say the least, I gave it a 'go'.

In her writings I came face to face with another spiritualist. It was reassuring to attend to the knowledge she shared, much of which sat well with me. However my soul was touched, tears rolled down my cheeks and I had to search for tissues when she wrote about a client who had had a past life as a rock. The experience made me realize I'd probably had a lifetime as a rock too. Though how one gets out of having a lifetime as a rock, I couldn't imagine. I was aware of several past lives; their reality had come to me at different times and in different ways. When considering this experience I could see how much sense it made – it explained my affinity for rocks. Yep, piles of rocks here and there, warmed rocks used for reiki, rocks for healing, for runes. And on a regular basis as we travelled here and there I'd be exclaiming to my husband about the wonderful energy that reached out from the rock walls which met us on excursions.

Being a rock seemed like a tame past life compared to others I'd had – like being burnt at the stake, or escaping the flooding of Atlantis. But maybe as a rock is when I learned patience, and to be stalwart, steadfast, dependable. This concept broadened my thinking of what a 'lifetime' could encompass – at least thousands of years, perhaps millions. Wow! I may be a very old spirit! Did I rest, during that time? Contribute? Claim? And …how I wonder, did my sojourn as stone end?

Live Better

At the centre of all things is an energy which is known by many names, I recognize it as God. This wisdom waits to be called upon, or asked for intervention. \s Intervention when **you** wish it, for you will not be pressured into any relationship which offends. On the other hand, you will be welcomed if you approach this wisdom.

Come often, come with the small stuff and the major happenings. You are always welcome to knock on the 'door', to come near for a prayer or for just a little chatter. In the meantime be careful where you go, and what you do. Be wise with whom you interact.

Do good.
Speak with regard.
Seek kindness, honesty and light.
Do what you know is thoughtful, right.
Live longer,
Live kinder,
Live better.

Look Ahead

Look ahead. There is no profit now in looking back. The past has brought you to this place; many lessons have been learned. The future gives opportunity to practice what your 'teachers' have taught and what you know you ought to pass along.

Look ahead, yet give thanks for the days which brought you this far. Yes, there is more learning ahead, but at this time it is your job to 'be' the person you have been becoming. This being, you, is loved, cherished, welcomed with the saints to the courts of heaven. Look ahead for the past cannot be undone, however if recompense is in order, undertake to make right that which you are able.

Examine self and see if different strategies are needed if communication can be heeded, understood and softly woven within the threads of daily living. Avoid anger which is indication of self-aggrandizement. Instead inquire if love be directed to and through you.

Look ahead, see peace welcomed where you live. Hinder not the growth which lies ahead, for you are on your way to becoming all that you can be, and that's enough as all can see.

Look Up, Give Thanks

And here you are with time to spare – a luxury in a busy life. You have time to give love, to give praise and to encourage the soul – yours and that of many.

Keep it up, it is needed. Things, it seems, don't always go well. Many are chided, put down, discouraged.

There is no need for discouragement. What is needed is a different point of view, a mind ready to seek change which lifts, anew.

Yes, look up. Yes, give praise. Look towards the sky not at your feet.

Yes, look up. Yes, give praise. Look towards the sky not at your feet. Look for language which is positive and up-beat. With attitude like this you'll bring sunshine to a cloudy day, you'll lift mind and soul.

Put on your smile, your sense of wit, and just go for it. God bless!

Look Within

Sometimes the world spins around us.
We seem to be attacked from many sides.
We are frazzled and exhausted, what can we do about it?

Look within – for there, settled in our soul is peace and
joy – far more than we would ever find without.

Allow the hurry, the prickles, the stabs and confusion to pass
by. Give them nare a thought nor be drawn in by them.

We are peace and love; this angst is not who we be. Let's
not get involved with it, but cut ourselves free. Let's find
within a quiet space even in the midst of a great foofaraw.

It's there, within, that we will see just who we
are and who we can be. With wisdom
We'll see what we should do and what is better left undone.

Love by the Barrel

Let's receive the love of the God we know, who sends it our way
by the barrel. Likewise let's be generous not stingy. We'll give
our head a shake - no more sending love out by the spoonful.
What does love look like?
How will I know that I've been blessed?
How will I know if I'm a blessing?
Enjoy the red hearts and happy smiles associated with love.
They're fun. Yet recognize love instead as kindness, acceptance,
good deeds, fair communication and thoughtfulness.
We'll open our heart to the whispers of understanding which float
our way; expand our kind thoughts and give them substance.
Thought is where love starts; compassion, perseverance
and willing heart and hands see it to manifestation. Accept
thanks and the feeling of well-being that accompany
your good deeds but look not for praise or adulation.

Love One Another

Love one another, be kind and tender hearted one to another. Confess your sins one to another, forgive one another and love one another as I would love you. I would have you know, my little ones, that I am your strength, I am your fortress, I am your guide.

Look not unto your own understanding, lean not on your own thoughts, lean not upon your own way of doing things, but lean on me. Lean upon me as you go through that which lies ahead. Learn to trust me fully for I am your God, I am your Stay.

Commit all your ways unto the Lord and your pathway shall be directed. Sing my praises freely. Do not worry about what others think of you, do not tarry but draw nigh for the time is short and time is drawing nigh when I shall come for my beloved – I desire that each of you will be ready when I come.

I love you as you are and where you're at. Stay close to me. I will make a way through the wilderness, I will give drink to the thirsty, and food to the hungry. Do not go ahead of me, stay close for I am the Living Water – whoever comes to me shall never thirst again.

Merry Christmas

"Ho, ho, ho and Merry Christmas"
We hear the cheery voice of Santa
as we walk through the shops with their
festive songs and ample offerings.

You, you, you.
A very merry year is wished for you
and for your family too.
May you all be blessed, set free of worry.
And confident that your best is more than good enough.

Know your intentions are seen and weighed,
Naught is found wanting,
You are welcomed with song and a smile.
Keep keeping on – a little here and there –
Or a lot, if that is claimed.
Go the extra mile, but from boasting refrain.

Mind a-Whirl

Is your mind a whirl?
Does it spin leaving you no chance to intervene,
or to make sense of the situation?

Step aside for a moment.
Relax. Think of the circle.

Like you the circle has no beginning and no end;
In it we see eternity, endlessness and ever being.

Allow mind to lasso the circle gaining wisdom with
which you face the day which is beginning.

Let your energy coast around the ever spinning frame,
Finding the inspiration you need today.

Wisdom abides within the heart of who you be.
And in that inspiration is a gift of tranquility.

Accept also the understanding and kindnesses which
are already yours, just waiting for the taking.

Minister to the Holy One

Take time to read the Word and to meditate on it, consider the impressions it bestows. For I, your God and Savior, am that word, and as you partake of the living bread you will feed on me becoming, daily, stronger and more wise.

Minister unto me. Strengthen me with the praise of your lips. You are mine; have I not chosen you from the foundation of the earth?

My Father, my Lord, you have filled me, you have filled us, with riches and precious treasures. Set our hearts aright so that our eyes may see the treasures you impose. Praise to your holy name.

I shall humble myself and seek your face. I shall listen and know your will for me.

In just a little while, I, the Lord, cometh in glory and in power. I shall not be held back. Watch therefore, and pray your garments may be found whiter than snow. Do not let them become tattered with the cares of this world. Keep them free from the sins of greed and malice, envy and bitterness. Buy from me oil, anoint yourself and be ready to feast with me for I have a spot reserved for each of you.

More from Life

Is life a 'drag'? Do you want more spice?
Or too hectic with no time for rest?
No matter which you find, my friend, there's likely more of the
same to come.
So….
Make a plan – sketch it on your calendar.
Stretch where you need stretching, close unnecessary or unwanted
patter.
Change your pace and where you focus time.
Correct your use of when and where you hide.

Life too dull? Find a group of well-doers who will welcome you in
joining them in caring for others, for the globe itself.

Do what you can to make this time, this place, an example of
kindness understanding and tolerance.

Never Wavering

Remember my child the words I have spoken to you, I have loved you from the beginning, and my love for you is forever – never wavering, never failing. Always steadfast, forever enduring.

My love for you is deep and never ending, it arrives from the Father, the Mother, from Jesus and others, often from those at home. You will know it when it arrives, just open your eyes, open your heart, and accept God's love – it's a love for all – and it's free!

This love is for all who are searching, looking and spiritually hungry; for in God there's a love satisfying and filling. You can give it away, but it always remains, and there's always more to share.

Come. Come my children, come drink of my love, I'll fill you to overflowing. Remember, my love is for taking and giving. I have called you out of darkness and into a world of light. Keep your eyes on me for I lead you on a straight path.

New Scenario

Forget that grumpy scene which brought you low. Think
instead of a gentle way to bring peace into this place.
Ah, yes. It may not be an easy claim, but you can do
it. You can raise the energy of this space. Look up. Feel
the love you need descend. Receive share, befriend.

Don't you feel better just contemplating this new scenario?

What you give will be returned in kind. Give well.

Let anguish no longer dwell within your heat. Be forgiven. Be well.

Accept this gift from Creation from the
one you may know as God.

You do? Feel spirit through and through,
for this Spirit dwells in you.

God bless. So be it.

No Defense

Sunshine crept around the corner,
Bit its way through envy and despair.
Made a place where light could reappear.

Darkness had no defense,
It couldn't override the gladness and happy hearts
Which appeared from nowhere.

Light had done it again,
It saw the change of heart it had provided
And the optimism that decided
To join in the display of joy and well-being.

No Heaven? No Hell?

Do not fall for the story that there is no heaven, no hell.

When you leave planet Earth, what you will experience in the Spirit realm will be what you have (so to speak) earned. Your experience will be dependent on your actions and intentions – and I must emphasize how important those intentions are.

You reap what you sow.

Hell, if that is what you'd call it, is a gross slimy, stinky abode for one who has had a life of greed, meanness or infliction of pain and/ or sorrow. If you ever find yourself there you might be able to ease out of the stench by changing your attitude and inclination even then. But that will be a slow miserable process. Remember this and make the changes needed even now, and on both sides of the change one knows as 'death.

Leave your pursuit of wickedness and self-gratification. Instead build a house of love, encouragement, life. Kindness dealt is kindness that will come back to bless you; as in patience, joy and forbearance.

No Pitty Party for Us

Let's look at blessings which have come our way,
some undeserved but gifted to us anyway.

Let's support the world of nature,
See its place in the starry sky, and in our future.

In the needs or joys of mankind
We'll continue being thoughtful, kind.

We'll be considerate of the ground we tred,
And considerate of those who walk beside
us, drag their feet or walk ahead.

We see the moon, the sun with assigned positions.
Without complaint they fulfill their obligations.

So…look past troubles which may worry you.
The birds do it and we can, too.

On Life and Living

We do not know the length of our life and whether our lives will be shortened by sickness or misadventure. Let's make the best of it!

A lot of stress was eliminated from my life some years ago, and with that it felt like years had been added to potential; I have had already more years than I thought I might. But even if I live to be old, feeble and as dependent once again as a child, or am taken soon, I make each day special, felt, enjoyed, accepted.

When I had those heart problems and was put on medications people said "How sad". But it was a turning point for me. I knew I had to really live each day that was given to me, and so I say "What a blessing."

Living each day does not mean that I'll be selfish or self-entered (though there are times I'm both of those.) It will not mean I'll be delighted with all that comes my way. But it does mean, and has meant, that I'll take time to savor awakening, soak in sunsets {and occasionally a sunrise), breathe deeply of the perfumed air in spring. Or of the salt-sprayed shore.

Part of living is experiencing cold, pain, hunger. But these only help us relish the cozy bed, simple meals and a warm relationship. When heart-sick (and I've been there) allow self to cry, fret, and hurt. Sob and howl, vent the brokenness. The salt in your tears will heal your spirit and sooner you'll be able to face life.

Well, it worked for me. It seems to me that each anguish comes with a set amount of grief. If we let it spill out it's used up faster. But smothered it will seep out slowly and seemingly forever.

Anger is a different matter. Usually we are angry if we don't get our own way. We are strong, determined. I'm still learning this one – lighten up! Most of the things that make us angry simply aren't worth it. Like…how important will it be ten years from now?

Let's divert the energy anger drags along into something useful – sweep the patio, dig in the garden, was the kitchen cupboards. Then, another time, quietly, gently, we'll talk over the issue that caused the anger; don't let it fester. On second thought, now, does it really seem that important?

One is Not Alone

We are surrounded by *All That Is*; this is the Great and Holy Spirit which lodges in me, in you, in all of life. It is the spirit that dwells with one, and is the comfort of us all.

We are not lost in the masses of humanity, kindness and charity, nor by the reality of darkness. Each of us is many, and each of us is one. I know it's possible, not sure how it's plausible, but heart and soul echo assurance of togetherness as well as the uniqueness of each one of us.

One Surrounded by All

We are surrounded by All That Is; by that one who
as Spirit sees us through and leads us on.

We're lead by kindness and charity,
moved by light not gravity.

Each of us is many, and each of us is one.
I know it's possible, not sure if it's plausible,
And ponder of a way to make it sound reasonable.

But heart and soul echo assurance of our
togetherness as well as of our uniqueness.

Therefore let us treat one another as family
See ourselves afresh not just one in the masses of humanity.

Let us look up and all around
Grasp the evolving that in each is found.

Our love and intention are paramount.
So let's do the best that we can
every day, each moment.

O

'Others' from Above

They've visited earth in times gone by,
They visit yet, we know;
These 'others' from above,
As well as those 'others' from below.

Causing concern, and with no invitation,
We see evidence of 'wise-men' visiting this plane.
Quietly, with flashing lights, intrepidly,
They come and come again.

We may declare them alien, a curse upon our land,
These beings of various agendas and temperament.
But they say they were here first, and planted us.
Take care - not all are benevolent or sublime.

Earthlings tell stories of visitors to Earth
Who left them in pain, confused, and in fear?
Who stole their progeny, left them in agony?
And if that is their intent, we don't want them here.

God we stand needing your wisdom and courage
Wanting peace and thoughtfulness from
ancient visitors who visit once again.
Wrap us in your cloak, keep us close we pray.

'Others' from Below

There are those who are prisoners of a bitter plan
who exist within this globe
I know them as 'the others below'.

That place is such a hell, they've left their bodies;
all that's left is just a shell;

Spirit's gravitated to a better place
there it finds compassion, and
there it's met with healing, love and grace.

If, 'what goes around comes around',
Which is, I understand, a law of this planet,
I'd hate to be a soul who easily
Took part in this conspiracy
Forgetting the cost of those in captivity.

God, our All in All,
forgive once more our wickedness,
our lack of respect, our carelessness.

Please set us on a path of righteousness
Help us overcome this crime we plead
And find a way to set these odd folk free.

Please Lead Me

I'm knocking at the door of truth, rattling at the heart of hope.
I'm waiting for the door to open, for love
to come a-tumbling forth.

Like you I seek an easy way to grasp wisdom and happiness.
Like me you'll find the door won't open until
our thoughts are kind and gracious.

Spirit cleanse, please, our thoughts
and our desires.
Wash us, set us out to dry.
Then lead us, please, to humbleness,
Knowledge from on high, and thoughtfulness.

Power Outage

Today the power went out for several hours. People arriving home to darkness, no heat, no operating machines grumbled and lit a candle or two. We felt we had moved backwards in time.

Ah, how heartedly we rely on that power and the power source.

This made me think of another power on which I rely too – the power of the Holy Spirit, the energy of God.

I thanked the hydro crew who got us up and running, then I gave thanks for the energy and wisdom bestowed by God, for my day is always better when I walk with angels and listen to their song.

Prayer to God

Guide me, oh Lord. Fill me with thy spirit.
Let your words, your thoughts flow through me.
May I this day, this night be a channel for the Holy Spirit?

My daughter, though wilt go forth in my name.
And I will go forth with you.
Do my will and you shall surely see great
and wonderful things come to pass.

Be not afraid, for where you are there am I also.
Abide in me and I will abide in you.
For as much as you love me and sincerely want to do my will.
So too do I want to fulfil your life.

Come, draw water from my well.
Thirst no more. I am with you always.
Unto you have I poured forth joy and
peace and a life of abundance.
Look unto me and I will heal your home,
your mind, your physical body.

The time is near when you shall see me in glory and splendor.
Be not afraid for have I not said I am with you always?
Yes, and I am with you this day, this night.
I will be glorified, continue to look to me.

Principles from Deuteronomy

We are ordinary people living in a time which is anything but ordinary. There is a new experience before us. Let's learn from negative experiences of the past and from hope within our soul.

We've been at this stage of evolution long enough. Be ready to be part of something new.

The world is before us; this is the land of the Lord which is to be shared anew. Form groups which will be accountable to one another and to the Devine. Choose overseers who are wise, who are impartial in the decisions they will have to make. Do not be afraid nor discouraged.

The God you know has brought you this far; part of the journey lies ahead but there is no rush. Follow the timing appointed, heed the still voice of Spirit.

Keep to your own tasks. Do not get involved in issues which are not on your agenda. Problems which seem too overpowering are no more difficult to overcome than the least of encumbrances. Stand. Fail not.

Privileged

We live in a busy world with many pulls on our time and energy. We need strength to keep going at work and home and places in between.

I find these hectic days give me opportunity to show tolerance and understanding. I'm not here for 'a good time' though that happens too. I'm here to see I've come a long way, but still have a way to go.

I'm getting there, wherever "there" might be. I'm learning to relax and enjoy the trip. And I'm experiencing loving every day both giving and receiving – I feel privileged to send some of that love your way.

God bless us all.

Punishment

Get over the idea that you are, or ever could be, punished by the one you know as God.

The Father's heart aches every time he witnesses your pain, he'd never harm you.

The Mother's mind tries to send you signals to set you straight – you are not singled out for punishment or shame.

What you experience is of another making – you reap what you sow. Your intentions in life are paramount.

Therefore spread a different form of 'seed' upon the globe. Choose a holy way of addressing he/she who wishes only your well-being.

Fall not into dark and wicked places. Seek out instead the good, kindnesses and eternal hope.

Planet Earth is charged with weighing your intent and paying you as your service and intentions permit.

Realization

There is likely in me, I'd have to say,
Some alien DNA.

Alien DNA?

Don't laugh, you can likely claim
Foreign places and the same.

In me the blood of the tribe of Judah resides
it would seem, and that of a Welsh princess,
gardeners, kings, an Asian queen,
and...at least one pirate.
What do you make of that scene?

Carpenters, preachers, teachers, seekers,
have left their identity in the person I be.
And I grasp the inevitability
Of having visited once or more in the galaxy.

We're a composite of this and that.
We come laden with history,
glorious times and misery.
We come with a spirit that's bound to find
The best it can be, this time around.

Really Living

Hi, God, I'm here. It's me!
I'm prepped, and willing to really live, to learn,
to teach, to revel in this glorious moment.

Forgive me if I laugh too loudly, cry spontaneously,
or seek a hideaway where I can regroup.

For what I see is fun, frolic, empathy and care.
But also there is sadness and an aching – everywhere.

Many know not that they are loved, accepted, cherished. They
feel left out, ignored, exploited. What do I say to these?

Kindness does not rise in every corner; in some greed and avarice
outweigh love - that's the result of the freedom we receive.

Freedom to make choices instead of living in a state of 'puppetry'.

"Do your best" – that's where it's at. Don't expect
perfection here today, yet see it making waves each day.

Remember Christ

Remember Christ, who was, like you, a spiritual being living in a human frame. Spirit within healed the sick, encouraged the down trodden, released the soul from the grasp of fear. Christ exhibits yet the model of what can be done by a spirit filled person.

He was crucified by those who did not understand the new way, the holy way. Ignorance and fear brought about the demise of thousands of thousands.

But of course they are not dead – you know that as do I. Know too the time of torture and of death to those who represent Spirit is at a close.

True wisdom is on the horizon. Move gently into this place. Move in with authority and love.

Your words will not always be pleasant to s/he who listens but they will be recognised as truth which directs the listener to a better way.

So be it. Amen

Remember the Words I Have Spoken

Remember my child, my friend, the words I have spoken to you. I have loved you from the beginning, and my love for you is forever. A love that is never wavering, never failing, always steadfast, forever enduring, a love deep and understanding, and a love you can trust and share.

This love that though you give it there's always more there. Kind of boggles the mind! But we find that's its true. Jesus, we thank you and give you praise.

I have called you out of darkness into light, I have put a watch on your feet to help you walk on the righteous street, staying away from harm and disbelief. Show forth my glory.

Remembrance

And who is this that knocks at the door of remembrance? It is he who treasures the many moments he and another cast their rods then pulled them in with faith and wonder, reunited.

It is she who sifts through the family album giving thanks to those who went before, to those who searched for understanding of nature, spirit, song, hope and service. In so doing they broadened their own capabilities as well as those of their spawn.

They learned the significance of positive thought, of diligent habits, of gracious speech. Through them, you too, in this generation, have learned as well.

And likewise, through you, your children learn and their children too, subtly, with no need for you to spell it out. Lead the life that leads to your gladness that your offspring follow in your footsteps. Then give thanks and praise to the one you may know as God.

Rhyme

This writing seems typical; God likes rhyme.
Spirit conjures poems from time to time.

There's something about it that calls attention
To that part of us that focuses intention,
On who we are and who we are becoming.

We are given opportunity to slouch or glow,
To interpret our condition and begin to grow
or not - if so inclined.

For Spirit is within, Spirit's light will shine.
And if we do what's good, what's right and kind. It will
be easier to believe that health is immanent this time.

And even if we don't act like saint or wise one,
God heals, cleanses, makes us whole if we ask,
believing, for that may be in our best interests.

Ring-a-ding-dong

Ring-a-ding-dong, ring-a-dong-dee
There's a wonderful spirit who visits with me.
A spirit who lets me know I'm special - just as I 'be'.

Spirit says just "go with it", learn along the way
And teach where you can in this ring-a-dong land.

It's not all heavy, but on the other hand, it's not all light.
There is darkness around. Avoid, take flight.

Cloak yourself with wisdom, as well as light.
Share with others who think you could be right.

Satisfied?

Your cat is satisfied with a simple life, with
food, water, a place to put its head.
It gives you thanks with a gentle purr,
Comes close and wants you near.
How sweet is that?
Does your cat's way help you realize that love is not necessarily
shared with gold, diamonds, and a fancy speech?
It is found in a gentle hand, a warm embrace, a smile,
kind words and that honest smile upon your face.
May God bless us all
as we take it upon ourselves
to make the best of life moment by moment.
Amen

See It Differently

When issues arrive that prove difficult, see if you can look at the situation differently. Meld strength and softness, focus with kindness at the helm, work quietly through the emotional side of things.

After that address the physical. Allow the help of others. Worry less. Perceive the outcome even as it unravels and you find you are surrounded with right concepts and the best possible conclusion.

Seven Principles of a Spiritualist

1. I recognize Divine Spirit, the All-in-All, the All that Is, whom I may know as God,
2. the Connection of all Life,
3. righteous Communication with, and Guidance from, the Spirit Realm,
4. eternity of Soul,
5. responsibility for my thoughts, words and actions. Making amends when I have harmed another, or have left undone that which ought to have been done,
6. consequences for my deeds according to God's Natural Laws - with Grace and Forgiveness meted as it has been offered,
7. and eternal progress open to me and to each of us.

Spirit, be in my mind, my thoughts and words I pray, as I go about your business - sharing holy wisdom with those who care what you might have to say and who may wish to concur. M

Sorrow

Consider sorrow to be a positive companion of growth. As you venture in to empathy and compassion, you may find yourself in an exhibition of sorrow; in doing so you aid another for you are bearing part of their hurt, their fear or anguish.

Cry with your friends, hold them close, and ease their burden by carrying some of the weight of their loss, their discomfort or distress.

Do not usurp the entire load of sorrow as some must be left for them; it will help them become the compassionate, receptive person they aim to be. And may God bless you both.

Spanking

I admit I spanked my children when they were disobedient, and gave harsh consequences for foolishness. To this day I regret so doing and wish these reprimands could be undone.

The children survived quite nicely it would seem, but I still wear an ache for having so behaved.

God, help us as parents to follow in your footsteps with kindness and love.

We Are the Window

We are the window through which we see the world unfold and through which others catch a glimpse of heaven.

Keep calm, shine bright, recognize that it is in you yourself that others catch a glimpse of the glory found in Spirit.

If this is so, and I believe it to be true, what changes must I make to give clear view?

Be steady in belief, do not waffle. Assure those who come in touch as you venture through your day that God is real – convince them not with clever words and phrases but by the life you live.

Then look through the window that you be, see others cleansed made whole. Watch them open up their window to view the grace and wisdom of personal eternity and love.

Spirit Whispered to Me

I am the God of each new day.
Let the problems, passion and the pain of yesterday pass on.

There's a fresh start for you today,
There's a new beginning every day.

As sun arises compassion, tenderness and
everlasting kindnesses are yours.
As skies lighten and sun moves from horizon, remember that I am
the God of Earth and of yesterday. And I am your God today.

Spirit Within

Spirit, you are here, within and without – always kind, considerate. You build up and do not tear down. You encourage us, yet set things right when that is needed.

You are honesty which is housed in love.
Within me is a part of that same spirit, that same knowledge, love and understanding.

I declare these things knowing your residence within my heart, humbled by your goodness, magnified by your wisdom.

I cherish your ability to work with and through me. I will let you, Spirit, shine that wisdom of yours through me to those who look for answers to the vagaries of life.

You are ever near, and always shining.
Thank you.

Still Together

We don't always agree,
My honey and me;
Sometimes we are downright rude
Though we try not to be.

God helps us find peace of mind
Through thoughtful response.
And caring for one another's concerns
Is something we both have learned.

Then together we float, together we fly.
We are caught up in ecstasy.
Splitting apart would injure each heart
So we muddle along, happily.

We open our eyes to the blessings we see
in moments of love and grace.
Then hand in hand we walk,
(still together)
Knowing we are in a good place.

(Eclipse 2011)

Strength in Kindness

Some people assume that their good deeds and kindnesses are an indication of weakness or lack of confidence. Not so!

It takes a strong, wise and thoughtful person to realize that they are making a statement to many as well as gifting one in need as they shell out of their time, energy or pocket and in doing so aid those who may never be able to return in kind.

> But they all will benefit in a myriad of ways from the courtesy of one who receives with thanks. Both the giver and receiver will be blessed. Be strong. Give in kindness, give generously with consideration.

Sunshine, not Storm

Be the sunshine, not the storm.

When dark thoughts seek you out and fear creeps near, choose
to be the sunshine, which will lighten up, mysteriously, the
space in which you dwell; the space which waits for you.

Be helped in a time of danger by calling out to the
spiritual realm. Those loved ones who have gone
on ahead have your highest good in mind.

Co-operation is part of the law of God. Seek and find
peace, wisdom, and a better realm. Inner wisdom
brings understanding, peace, confidence, serenity and
an awareness of your true and everlasting power.

Love is the permanent force, for love rules all.

May my eyes be opened to the spiritual entities
who work with me with good intention.

Wanted: one who offers service, co-operation, and harmony.

Heal the sick. Awaken souls who are ready.

We are accountable for what we do, not for what others do.

Be, with me, a breath breathed together. You are never
alone, but are encompassed by those who love you.

If you seek to serve you will not stumble without
receiving means to raise yourself.

Redeem self when it has faltered. You get another chance.

Duality that leads to unity is complimentary.

Love is always stronger than death.

The power of Spirit is greater than the power of matter.

Faith born of knowledge provides a good foundation.

Weary not at service for it is the centre of love.

Touch the souls of those that are ready to be awakened.
Only persons themselves can convert themselves.

Synthesis

Let us create possibilities by visualisation, discrimination and non-attachment as we apply ourselves and look for wise results.
Let us determine what we have learned, and what next needs be acquired. We prepare for what lies ahead.
Temptation to procrastinate will be put aside and we will synthesise new understandings with what already stands within. Sensitivity and sensible will be balanced. A good dose of common sense will be applied. We will press onward with good cheer avoiding pitfalls which may present themselves.

Temple of God

Allow the patter of a different ilk
Define the song you sing today.

Leave the known voice or chatter.
Let Spirit have its way
In tongue or tone you may not know.

In doing so, you then allow
The Holy Spirit to have a say, to influence you from head to toe, to
build the temple that you be, the temple which God already sees.

What can we say but halleluiah and 'hurray'
for the Great Spirit chooses to lodge
Within the temple we're seen to be.

Thank You

Thank you for the things you do which
touch a heart or lifts a soul.
You think no one sees the kindnesses you do.
But I see them says the God you are learning to know.

For even if you know not me
I know and love you says the one who gave you
breathe; who watches daily over you.

You are loved, treasured, held in high esteem
Just because you be, and just because, as Spirit, I love thee.

In our universe we are just a dot. But on that dot we rely.

The Fire of Life

Life is not a bland safe occurrence. It is a place
with the call of children, the demands of a
spouse, the expectation of the community.

Do what you can in a range which is governed by
common sense. Set aside time for quiet contemplation
as well as for the business of work and play.

Set aside energy for games, joy, and exercise. Include love
in all you do. Include the stranger – with caution- look for
right thinking and kind ambitions, holiness and grace.

Be discreet in what you say and what you do.
Yet speak with honesty and kindness,

The Globe Changes

The world we know, this globe, is going to change – in fact it will be hard to recognize. We will have to change too, if we are to there dwell. Let's be ready to take on a different form (or lack of form) and a different way of being.

Be ready to adapt. Be wise.

Consider the past, how at one time this sphere was a ball of ice, another time was host to monstrous beings of voracious appetites with fearsome claws and teeth. (Except for their good looks they really had no redeeming attributes.)

If you are to remain upon this land you'll need to choose a different form a different style. Be ready for this, but don't expect it for a while. Be flexible, forthright, kind, wise.

Be one who clears the way with recompense and stays away from pride. Be one who looks ahead, realizes things won't stay 'as is'. Dodge the hypocrite, embrace the meek, allow Spirit to supervise.

THE NEW REVELATIONS
of Jesus Christ

God has given unto his people knowledge and visions of that which will take place shortly. He has encouraged me, his handmaiden to pen a book of consummation. God bears witness to the testimony of the Christ, her 'older brother', Jesus. Together they bear witness of what is yet to come.

Blessed are you who read this message and who heed what Spirit has to say. This message is not for a few but is for all those who love the Father, Mary the Mother, and the saints who, sometimes at great expense, even the loss of their bodies, have been faithful to the love placed within. Be blessed, be wise, and be humble before the God you know for time is of essence.

Grace to you, and peace for all, and love without measure to those who have, to those who continue in the faith and to those who at even the 'eleventh hour' accept and heed what Spirit shares. Everyone is welcomed, accepted, drawn close.

My heart was heavy as I drew close to look upon the Earth. I'd despaired about the rancor, the greed, the unkindness and blasphemy; I did not want to draw near.

But behold, my visage was overwhelmed with the goodness I saw, the love that was extended in a real way to those less fortunate, to those lost, wandering through the streets, overtaken with hopelessness.

I saw crowns upon the heads of those who had made it their mission to do good and no harm, to those who had included the planet as well as the people in their world mission. The vibration of the earth settled, heart beat stabilized and with good intention we welcomed aboard all those who had made this choice, even though in some instances it had been beyond them in the physical realm but was embraced in the spirit.

Watch. The Christ comes; and comes from the skies - comes for all who believe. These beliefs may differ person to person, but if they are seated in love, in compassion and righteousness, the I Am, the All in All, the one who was, and is and yet will be, the beginning and the end says, "Come. Come, you are welcomed."

My heart was stirred, my mind put at the disposal of the Christ. I heard a gentle voice, say 'Welcome. Welcome indeed. You have felt left out, abandoned, overwrought, maligned and used in trying fashion. Let me erase those hurts, let them be replaced with joy, understanding and boldness in your acceptance of what lies within. For you are magnificent – I mean – just the way you are. You are magnificent, made pure, holy in the sight of God and of all. You are without spot or wrinkle. Avoid evil or even the appearance of evil, instead focus on what is pure, is wholesome and of good report. Be especially careful of this in the presence of the young – give them no reason to harden their heart.

An inner voice said 'write this', I bowed my head and listened to the one I know as God.

I felt humble and out of my depth, but God said, 'Not so. I choose who I do, and today I choose you.' (My eyes could not hold the tears that came; so I blotted them, blew my nose and continued with the message.)

Feed the hungry, lift up the broken hearted, do good in a way that does not take power from the one you help. Be cognizant of differences yet accept as is. Do not be hollow, but be filled with compassion which spills over in smiles, kind words, finances, and a place to lay their head. Be hospitable, you may harbour angels.

At the core of all you do or say there should be love. When it seems in short supply, welcome an ample delivery of infinite supply, love knows no end. Accept also, from Spirit, a gift of discernment so that you will have clarity of understanding, of knowing what should be ignored, cast out, or embraced. Our good works are seen; we are rich in strength, foresight, deliverance and avoiding harm. And what harm can there be to one who puts trust in God? For even if the body is mutilated and appears dead, the soul is alive and well; it is delivered from the mayhem of earthly troubles and is content, at peace with the saints. Therefore put fear behind you, be instead at one with the Oneness that has no beginning, no end.

Do not be part of the wickedness that intrudes upon the communities of Gaia. Keep clean; protect babies, children, the old, and the infirm. There is no good in putting before your eyes desperate and wicked visions. Put a watch on your mouth and shine a light upon your soul. Do good. Harm not. Be holy, but do not aggrandize your 'holiness'.

Walk a path you'd want your grandchildren to walk. Talk a story that could come from the mouth of an innocent child. Remove pain and sorrow from the hearts of others as you are given grace to so do. What you do will come back and be done to you, for as you say, 'what goes around comes around'. This is a law of living on planet Earth. Heed it wisely.

Do not give in quickly to lusts of the flesh but seek wisdom and act accordingly. Be blessed with honor, health and kind deeds. This is not to say you should not desire your partner, new clothes, gold, diamonds or whiskey; no, nor song and dance and loud laughter. In the right time and place these are all magnificent gifts. I saw children draw nigh, and angels mingled with them. They looked up, pointing to the sky, a soft light settled on them all. 'Come close, be holy, even as these' encouraged an ancient master. They did, and brought many to this gentle place. Kindness was in their hearts, and kind words upon their lips. In small groups they met as family might for they recognized themselves, indeed, as one.

The earth began to shake and stars fell, but the people raised their hands and commanded the shaking to cease, the stars to stay in place. And so it was - grace, faith and righteousness prevailed. The stars flew back into the heavens; the earth became quiet and welcoming. The people and angels fell upon their knees, giving thanks. The perfume of roses filled the air in a blessing from Mother Mary. Then a trumpet sounded; it was a song of victory; victory in the triumph of wholesomeness and kindness over despair and disease, of righteousness and cleanliness of heart over disrespect and wantonness.

Let us, the people said, write a new code upon our hearts, new phrases for our lips. Let us humbly follow the nudging God provides for each - within. To this they did agree and this they did.

The energy some know as God looked upon the scene. Who'd have 'thunk' it? God proclaimed. I have to give these people credit. They've taken a mess, turned it around and are headed now in a holy direction. And so it was, and so it is, and so shall it be ever thus, unless of course, some day it is not.

The Song Within

There is a song for us to sing –
A song that dwells within;
Hear the tune, feel the beat.
Tap it with your heart, your feet.

Note the promise of forbearance,
The despair in omnipotence.
For we are one, one which has infinite attributes.
You be some of these and I do too.

The song is for us all
Even if it meets one to one
or one to none at all.

Let's put aside our differences,
Focus on our needs and wishes.
Join with others in the harmony
Of honouring individuality.

Thoughts

Things that seem hard become easier as you point self in the
right direction and walk with strength. You are not judged
as you thoughtfully walk through this, your journey.

When turmoil hits your life or the world in general, let things fall
into place, you are affected by what goes on around you. However,
don't 'wear' it. Hunger to help the world dwell in harmony.

You are the answer God puts forth, for you have thoughts
of hope, peace, love and good will. Care for others in
your own way. You determine how you, even in a small
way can advance kindness, and a clean environment

Send out righteous thoughts. Your thought is like a pebble
dropped in a pond where the energy goes out in waves.
Little by little changes begin and an awakening evolves.

Accept the courage offered unto you, courage to act in peace.
Share your light, wisdom, charity. How you love self and others
in the world is the most important thing that you can do.

Together All Are One

The light we see is, was, and continues. Likewise we are, were, continue. No end, no beginning, but energies that mingle, co-mingle, be. This is God, and this is you and me.

Think not it is you only, for those who are, were, will be, are also part of this mingling. Together we are one. I am, you are, we be.

Together we occupy this realm of time and space. But also we occupy a realm that knows no end but whose limits are boundless.

The 'be' we are, the thoughts we think, the choices made extend outside ourselves to the corners of this universe – and beyond.

Every choice we make has a ripple effect within and without. Therefore let us choose wisely and with love.

Transparency

There is no place in heaven or on earth where God is not.
The energy of God is the glue that holds it all together.

The kindness of God, working through our hands heals the world.
The strength of the Father, spoken in our
encouraging words, lifts the stranger.

Let the Light of God within shine through.
May that Light shine honestly in all we do.

'Own' the energy within.
Let it lead us to the place we want to be,
The place where we dwell with God
And dwell with God in a state of transparency.

Treasures

I accept peace and the light of one I know as God.
I accept gifts of health, love, abundance.

May these be the treasures I'll defend,
For in this light I recognize truth, goodness, and kindness.

Ultimately it is love that speaks volumes.
It is love that will bridge my way past time
to a reunion with the Almighty.

I will not be defensive for there is no need to be so.
I am loved, protected, just because I am family.

At the altar of God I am accepted, loved, cherished.
Here I find wisdom, kindness and the refreshing of intention.

So be it, for me, thee, and all who so choose.
May we see and express your vision.

Triumph

Sometimes we find ourselves in a battle
of our making;
a thought or a remembrance tries to pull us
down. What to do? Where to turn?

Let's step up – ask for light
which enables us to do what's right,
to look anew, to see with vision.
Then… listen.

By stepping up to a higher place
wisdom is gained;
apply it generously.
Step up once more – and from this height
give thanks that Spirit is in charge again.

Love will keep you going and day by day
you'll find yourself in peace,
day by simple day you'll triumph
over the weight that tried to pull you down.

If it knocks on your door once more
you know just what to do,
take upward steps
where spirit friends route for you.

Troubles

Pain and suffering play a part in our growth and understanding – we learn through it. Troubles prepare the heart and let the soul rise.

The steps we take as we go through troubles are the ones that take us where we are to go. Let us never judge self harshly, nor judge the AllThatIs.

Remember we have power to change, and in doing so we gather wisdom which one day we will be called to share with others. And one day we will see the strength we gained by going through this ordeal.

Underpinnings

Life is better with strong underpinnings – those structures, and that foundation which will capably support in storm or inclement weather.

As a family who looks out for one another we will have a firm foundation; for those of us not related, we too can design a system which brings us into a similar supporting 'family'.

By supporting one another we increase our chance of success for each and plausible living for all.

Make the way clear for everyone to succeed who honours truth, diligence, hope.

For those who know not this better way, comfort, correct, sustain. Give them the support which flows through you, so that they too can become the caring person which resides within.

Upheaval

We've seen interesting changes lately in social mores and in some a transition to lack of sensitivity – the old 'tell it like it is' enigma. Change is something we expect and work around or perhaps cheerfully embrace. Gaps are plugged, other options are opened freely and our forward motion needs acquire thoughtfulness and right intent.

Water seeks out a path of least resistance, and we could follow its determined path. If soul is not careful, if it does not focus on upward growth, it could find itself settled in a dank, dark hole.

It will take determination to find strength, to oust greed, slothfulness and lack of kindness. But this is what we are called to do, and what we indeed will do. For there will be upheaval of the globe, its crust will crack, adding to the dismay of want and lack.

Rumbling will occur within the sea, and within the heart. Do what you know is best, what you know and can trust. Call on Spirit, on the God of your youth, call on the All-in-all whose love never left. In this mad confusion find peace, strength and a light that will guide you into doing what is right, what is wholesome kind, polite. Manners go a long way in a crisis and at a time like this.

Waiting has Rewards

Do you 'champ at the bit', so to speak, when you miss the bus, don't get on the ferry of choice, or find yourself unable to reach a goal?

Fuss a little, if that makes you feel better, then analyze the situation, make a plan for 'best use' of the gift of a quiet, peaceful interlude.

Settle your thoughts on the gentle heart within; let its love encroach upon the brittle parts of self, softening our demands, limiting frustration, and giving us a fresh perspective.

Consider the 'synchronicities' which have happened of late, which now you realize, are more likely sent with divine grace.

Appreciate the situation, give thanks, and wait.

Walk Tall

Let's walk through life with our eyes open.
Let's make a note of the path which leads to love and freedom.
Let's avoid the path that drags one into crime and an untimely fall.

There are open spaces for us to explore.
There are green places where we shall thrive.
Our view will be open, our options many;
for we sing a happy song, we see love for all.

In our heart, at the base of righteousness, we choose to dwell,
We'll live there with a song and a smile.
We may start at first with small steps but
soon we'll stride with honor.

Through it all, we'll walk tall.

We Are God's Be loved

Behold my children, you are my beloved. I truly love you – just as you are. I love you, I have called you to show forth my praise. I have made you for my glory and honor.

You will go forth with my name on your lips and my praise in your hearts. Show forth my love to your neighbours, your friends and your sisters.

Know that I love them and give freely my love. You have need of rest my little ones. Bring all your cares to me that my resurrected life might be known in your life. Give me your cares and anxieties and my resurrected power will be in your life.

I am your source there is no other. I know how your hearts are, many of them are heavy, I would have you know you can bring everything before me. Share what is deep in your heart so I can set you free, so your spirit can be free to soar above every problem.

I love each of you just the way you are and see great things in store for you. I love you deeply, I love you all.

We Are the Window

We are the window through which we see the world unfold and through which others catch a glimpse of heaven.

Keep calm, shine bright, recognize that it is in you yourself that others catch a glimpse of the glory found in Spirit.

If this is so, and I believe it to be true, what changes must I make to give clear view?

Be steady in belief, do not waffle. Assure those who come in touch as you venture through your day that God is real – convince them not with clever words and phrases but by the life you live.

Then look through the window that you be, see others cleansed made whole. Watch them open up their window to view the grace and wisdom of personal eternity and love.

We Live in God's Wisdom

Let us open our hearts; let it be the space where we
listen. Let's give thanks as we live in God's wisdom.
We'll be grateful, expectant – not frozen in time,
For we are connected to the divine.
We are beloved, part of an expanding family.
We will be of good cheer – for all we need is given - amply.
We have the light, health, finances and joy we need.
Our strength and loving outlook are guaranteed.
Thank you Spirit; yes, thank you indeed.

We Want to Change Our Ways

Lord God, who is merciful as well as righteous, please show us how we can look up, look past dismay, and in doing so carve a path which takes us to a holy place.

Show us, please, step by step, how we can leave behind foul language, mean plans and worrisome behaviors that we reveled in knowing not what we should do.

We know we have done wrong, we want to change our ways and even our thoughts – from whence comes action or lack of action.

Please show us step by step, one day at a time, how we can see afresh and learn to live a wholesome loving life.

We thank you for a second chance (or maybe our third or fourth) for our aim now is for kindnesses to all, and a righteous walk.

Whistle Your Own Tune

Sun creeps through venation blinds.
I draw the curtains and lift them.
It's Wow! to a wonderful day
As a tune erupts from within.
I whistle that tune,
And hammer the countertop
With a zingy tap, tap.
I get my body involved with the beat. and a mop.
Energy climbs and drops, does it again;
Love of living bursts forth.

I'll remember, of course, this moment in time,
It's a beautiful day for such sport.
I'll whistle that tune for many a moon,
And smile while I do.
If you'd like to join me
Well…you are welcome, too!

Who Am I?

And who, Maureen, are you to think you should speak on behalf of Spirit? Who gave you the right?

With humble heart I reply; I'm an aspect of the Holy One, mostly Spirit, partly flesh, I'm a handmaiden of the one I know as God.

I take this calling seriously but also know the lightness, kindness and love this 'duty' provides.

Come spend some time with us - meaning me and my guides, see if these words, this way, will work too, for you, and may God bless us all.

Millar

Wicked Intentions

Be aware. You are living at a time when pockets of darkness abound, when Earth ignores the stench of greed and power.

To provide a better environment for yourself and loved ones resume an interest, execute kindness and compassionate thinking.

Do not return to barbarism and aggression; it is better to leave the planet than to aggrandize wicked intent.

Begin with gratitude for those things that bode well, chip away at moderate infringements. Subject wicked intentions to more than sporadic involvement but to its overthrow.

We Are the Window

We are the window through which we see the world unfold and through which others catch a glimpse of heaven.

Keep calm, shine bright, recognize that it is in you yourself that others catch a glimpse of the glory found in Spirit.

If this is so, and I believe it to be true, what changes must I make to give clear view?

Be steady in belief, do not waffle. Assure those who come in touch as you venture through your day that God is real – convince them not with clever words and phrases but by the life you live.

Then look through the window that you be, see others cleansed made whole. Watch them open up their window to view the grace and wisdom of personal eternity and love.

Winds of Peace and Change

Let the winds of peace and change lead
us in a way which works for all.

May it work for the globe herself, the skies,
and the planets of a different realm and time.

Instead of trying to unwind similarities, let's adopt a view
which cherishes uniqueness as well as similarity.

Let us give way to the song within
Which ever reverberates in you and me.

Yes, in us as well as in the birds, the bees
the plants, the air, the salty seas.

Wisdom and Understanding

Learn from your parents. Learn from experience.

Learn from pondering. Learn by practicing.

You may be learning what to do, or 'not' to do. You can determine what would be a better way for the driver, the parent, the teacher. Then you can apply it when you are in the 'driver's' seat.

Consider that which brings about peaceful understanding. Do you notice how it helps when questions are asked? When you are involved in the undertaking? Are there places in your life even now where you could be the one asking those thought provoking questions?

Keep your ears open to hear past the words said. Note demeanor, stance, composure of the body. What works? What stirs up trouble? What brings consideration to the front?

Is it a quiet calm voice? What outcomes are observed with different language and tone? There's a lot to be learned that will enhance your life and the lives of those nearby. So keep your ears open, watch with those eyes. Little by little you become wise.

Who am I?

Some call me Mom, or Momma, Mummers,
Grandma, wife or friend. I'm Maureen to many, Mo
to a few, and daughter to the God I know.

I recognize Spirit as the voice that leads and teaches,
that keeps me in the loop and keeps me close.

I find some time to meditate, to look within
my heart and listen to my soul.

With quiet time and pen in hand thoughts make it
to this page. I consider it a present to us all.

I'm recognized as Spiritualist for I understand
that I'm eternal spirit, as are you.

Presently, of course, having a human experience is what we do.

Past lives that I recognize and messages from loved
ones who've gone ahead teach me that I'll never
really die - there's no such thing as 'dead'.

Aim High

Aim for the highest form that resides within.
End distinctions of race, colour, and belief.

Catch a glimpse of the world that can be.
Seek light, knowledge, wisdom and spiritual truth.

Hold on to what is precious, what is right.
Learn to sift fact from myth.

Add consideration and guidance from above.
Comfort those who mourn
Who need sustenance and love.

Undo the wrong that you have done;
Where possible make amends.

Add service to your fellow man
And to animals that need your care.

Open your heart, your eyes
For there are opportunities out there.

Be blessed as you are a blessing.

Were You There Too?

No one talks about it much, but I have a hunch
that I've lived on a planet or two.

As I rested in a meditative trance
The dreams that I had and places that I've seen
were not of this time, nor of this plane.

If this rings a bell, and you say, "I know that
feeling well", I'd love to hear from you.
For you've probably been with me in the Pleiades,
Or made serious trips afar.

Were you there when we spun flax into cloth, wore
sandals, followed in the footsteps of the Nazarene?

When he was whipped and placed in the tomb,
wasn't that the worse thing you'd ever seen?

And who'd of guessed that he would reappear
As Spirit where he could lead us in the way that we should go?

But now we know; and Spirit is close, so...
let's share this info with those who, like us, would
benefit from hearing this good news.

Wisdom Within

There is a part of us, deep within, our spirit, that wants to praise the Lord. If that part of us is to grow, it must be exercised.

As an athlete must practice day in and day out (consider the long distance runner) and on rainy days as well as the sunny, so must we practice praising – through hard times as well as through blessings.

As we daily strengthen the praise part of our being, it will be built up so that we will not falter when the 'going gets tough'. We will be carried through tribulations still praising our Lord.

Praise can become as much a part of our day (and hour) as is prayer or partaking of God's word.

There is a part of us that hungers to praise our Savior, our God. Only by opening our hearts and mouths and letting praise come forth will that void, that hunger, be filled.

Therefore let us set our minds to praising the Father, Jesus the Son, and the Holy Spirit. Let us exercise a vital part of our being.

Wretchedness

Many live in a state of wretchedness – some because of poor choices they have made, but others are in this state because of unfortunate dispersal of the necessities of life.

Poverty results from unbearable paucity on the one hand and unreasonable riches on the other.

Fair and equitable opportunity should be available to all. Living in squalor with lack of hope or wholesome foods begets more of the same. This chain needs be broken and replaced with fairness, kind intent, and discipline.

There is plenty for each; therefore let us open our heart and eyes for ways we can mend this broken system.

We replace greed with love and kindness or reap the dark consequences.

Underpinnings

Every life has its ups and downs which are arranged as learning and teaching mechanisms. To make the most of these experiences it is wise to have your underpinnings, that supporting structure, that sincere foundation fashioned in such a way that it is strong and secure.

As a family who looks out for one another you have this advantage. Design a system which brings together like-minded friends and neighbours who need such backup. By supporting those who do not have these advantages you increase for all the chances of success and plausible living.

Make the way clear so that everyone can succeed who honours truth, diligence, hope. And for those who know not this better way, comfort, correct, sustain. Give each the support they need so they can exhibit the caring person who resides inside.

Writing Opportunity

For many years while praying or meditating, Maureen Millar was given poetic messages by the one she knows as the Great and Holy Spirit, or as God. As time went by she was encouraged to put these thoughts together in a book, and to include pictures she had taken. (And a couple her husband took of her), The thoughts and visuals were to be shared with others. Her daughter Robyn added photos and her artistic strengths, and **Inspired by God** was published. More inspiration led to another book, *Still*, **Inspired by God** which has also gone through the publishing line up and is now available widely as a Kindle or paperback. (Both books are available through Amazon and your neighborhood book store.)

As she penned additional writings under the title **Inspired by God's Wisdom and Peace** Maureen was prompted to include in her next book the spiritual writings of others who know, too, the same Source. This is where you may come in.

Have you written spiritual messages which have yet to see the light of day? They congregate in dusty corners instead of shedding their light? You may include your works in your own section in the next book if you think they'd fit under the title of *Together*, **Inspired by God**. This is an opportunity for all of us. Contact maureenmillar@shaw.ca, if you have inclination or questions. Maureen

Zion, Heaven Await

Printed in the United States
By Bookmasters